Use this practice book four time
your 3-8 year old to help them better the fine motor skills needed to master handwriting. Practicing penmanship and letter formation can not only help children lean their letters and the alphabet faster but also helps them have an easier time learning to read and spell.

It is suggested to use large crayons , thick markers, or a large pencil for better development of the fine motor skills, as well as making the process more entertaining for your child.

Juju Journals

Jot down your thoughts

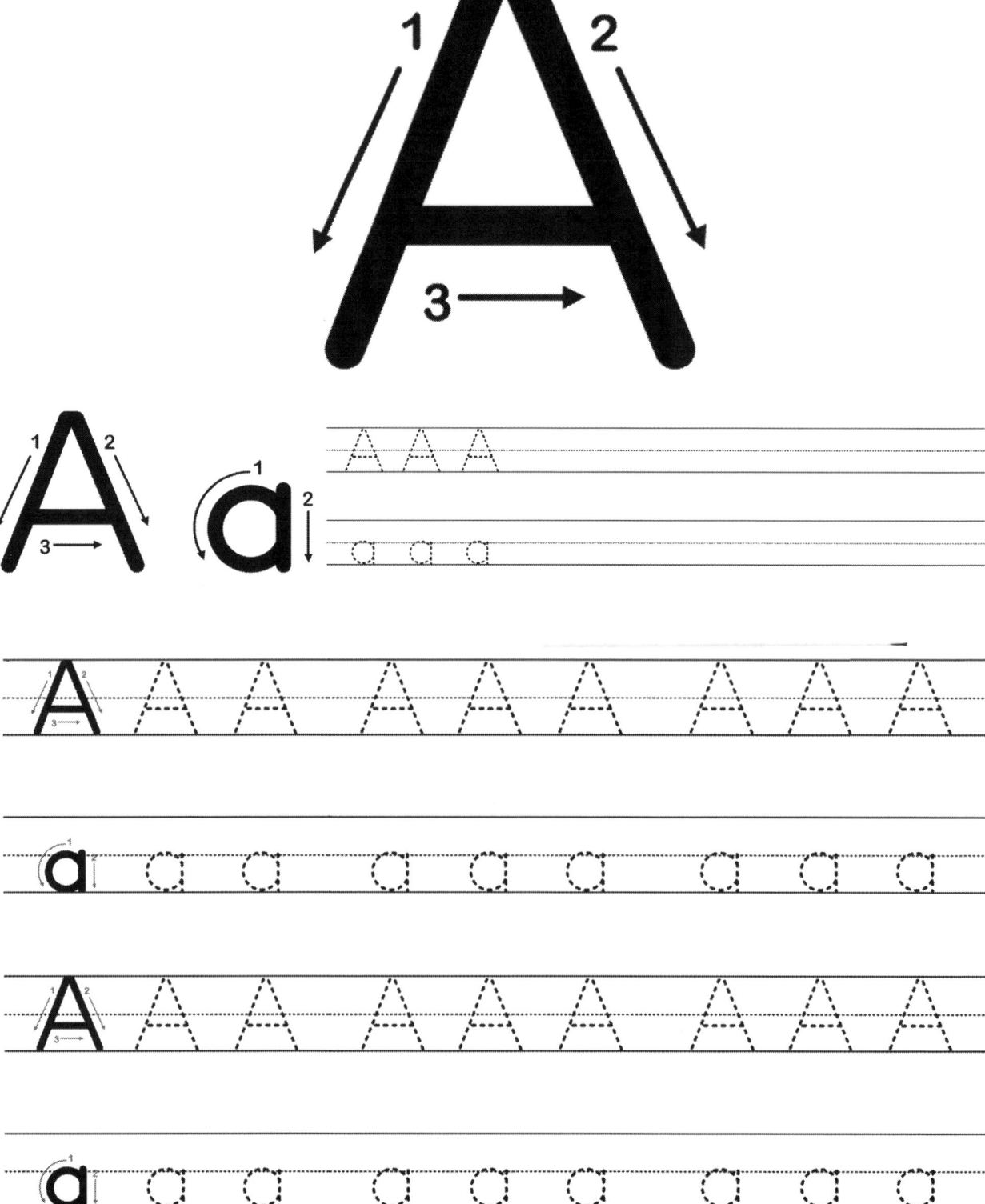

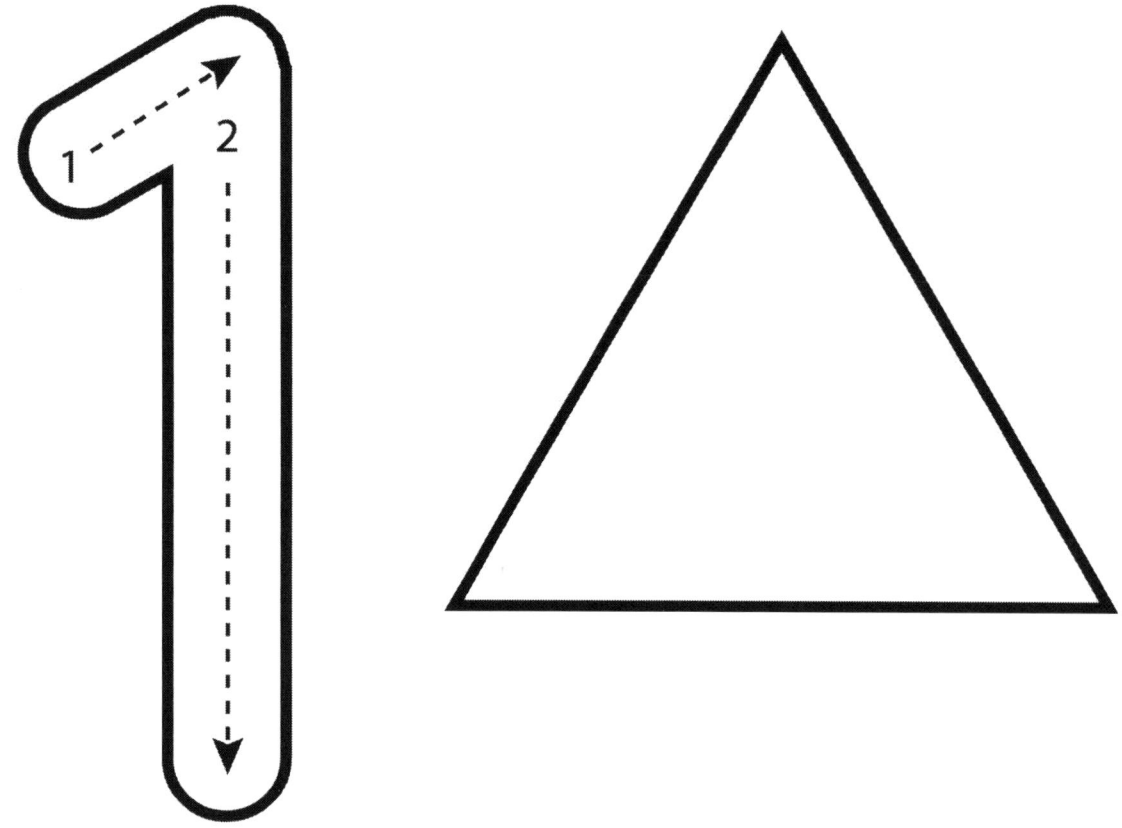

one

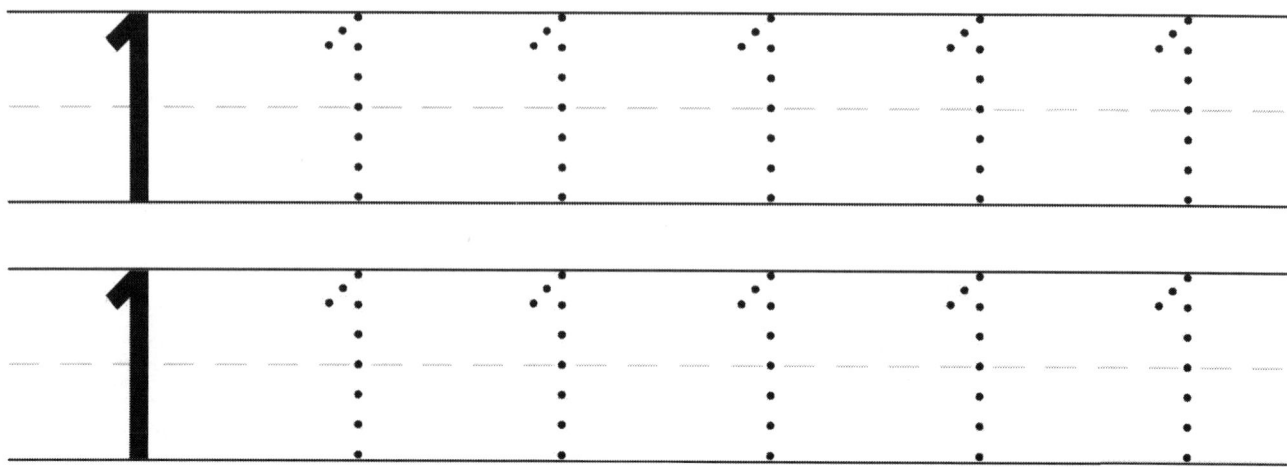

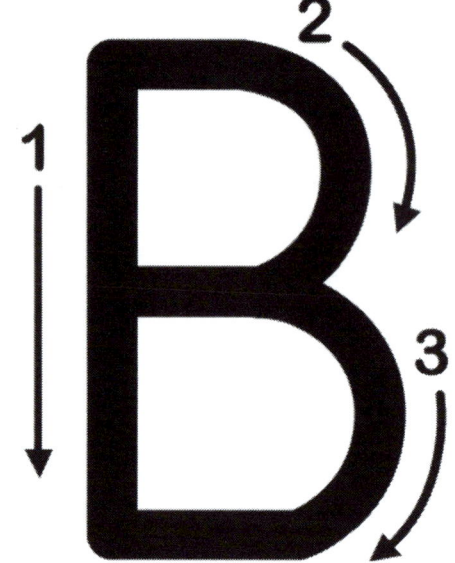
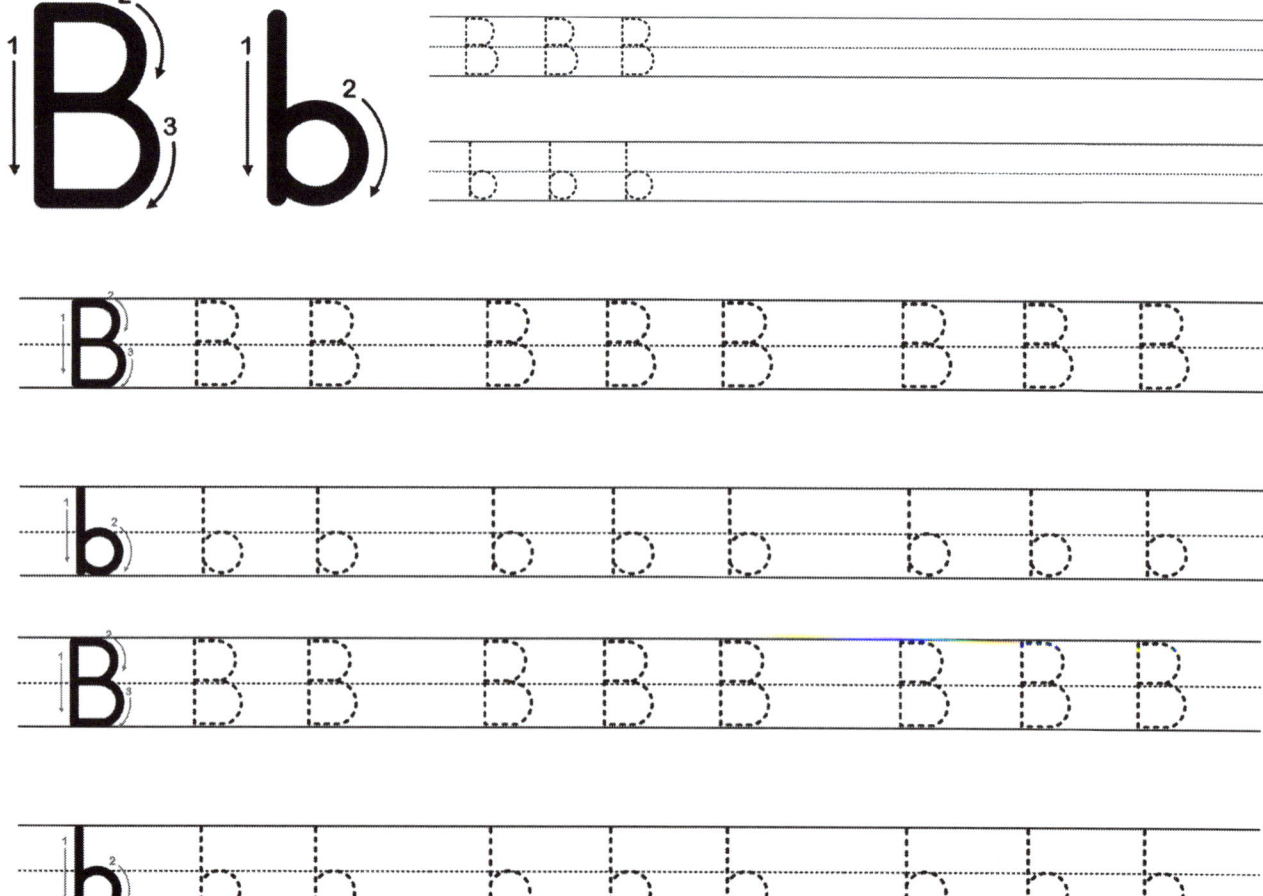

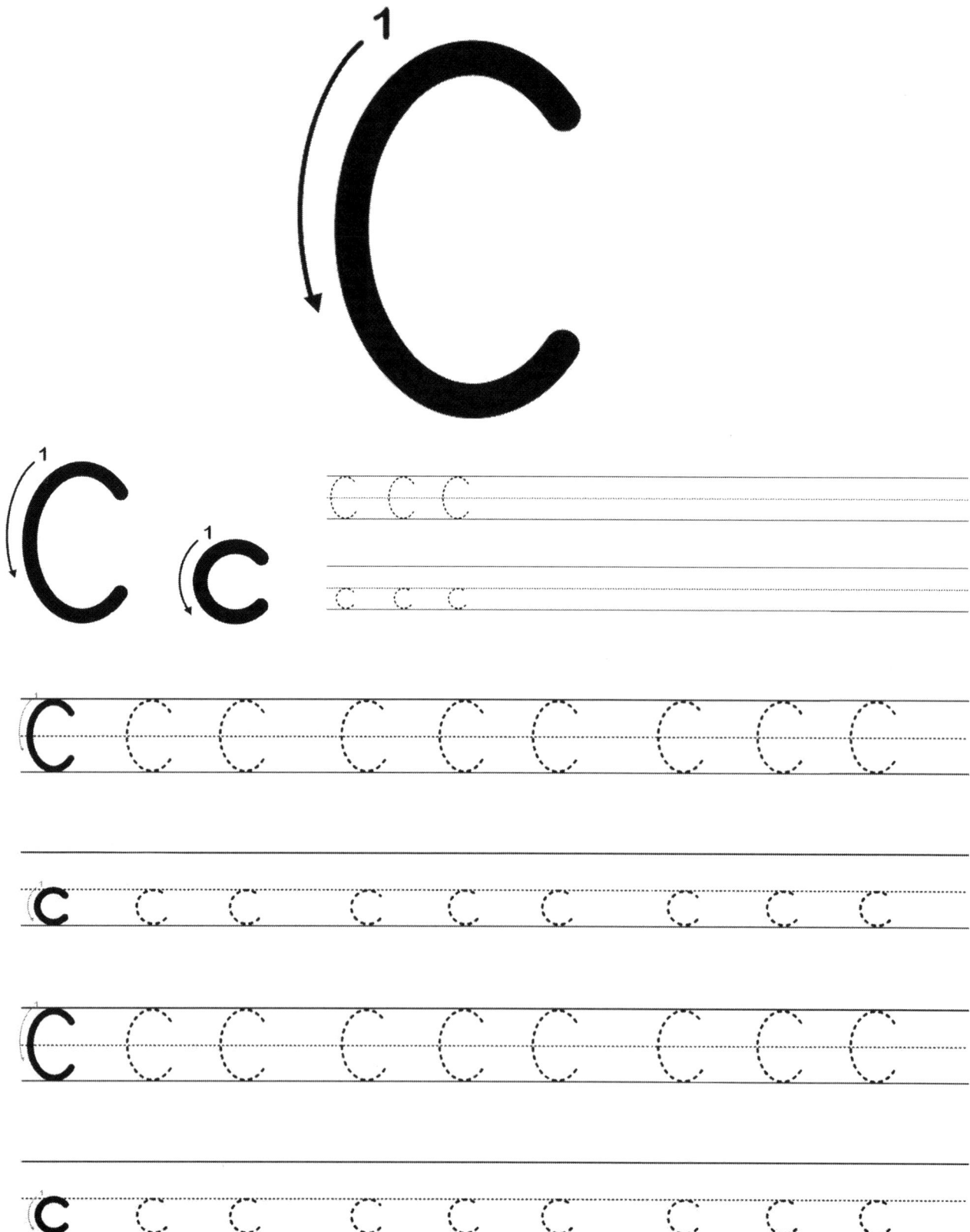

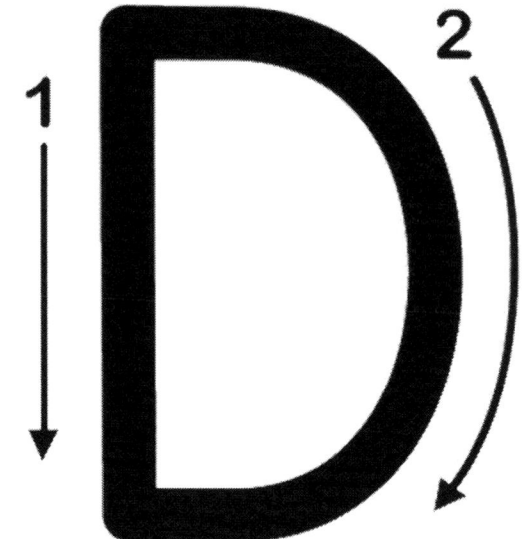

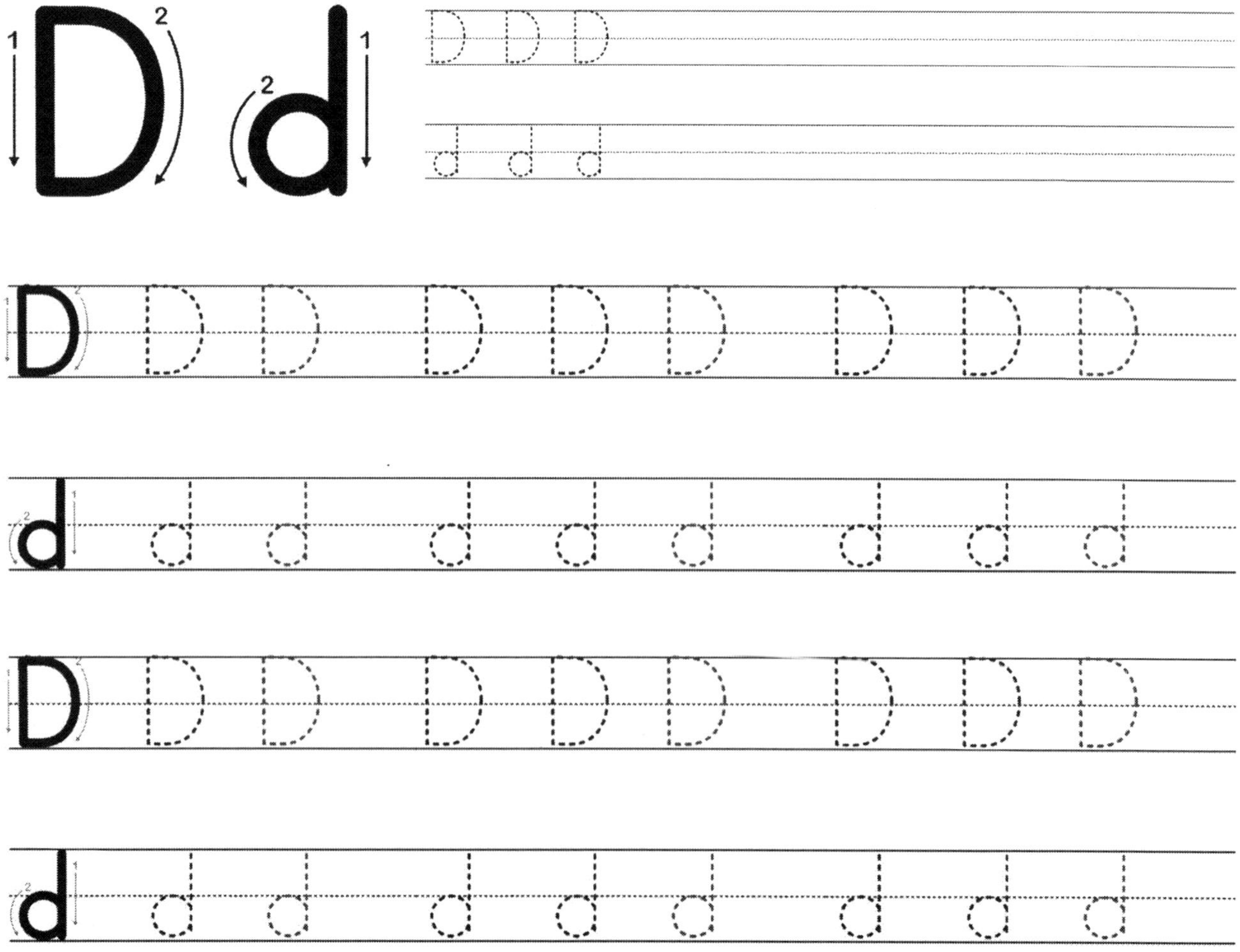

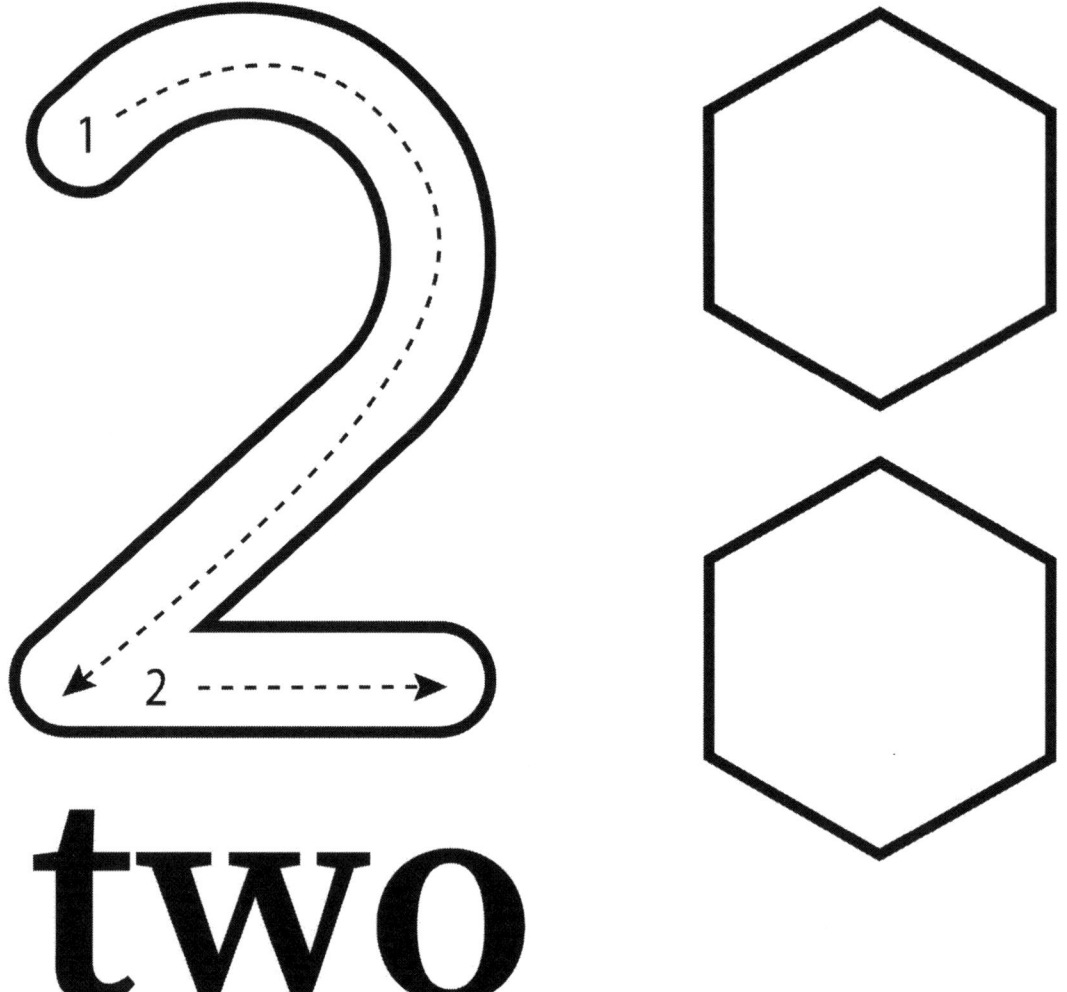

two

2	2 2 2 2
1	1 1 1 1
2	2 2 2 2
2	2 2 2 2
2	2 2 2 2
2	2 2 2 2

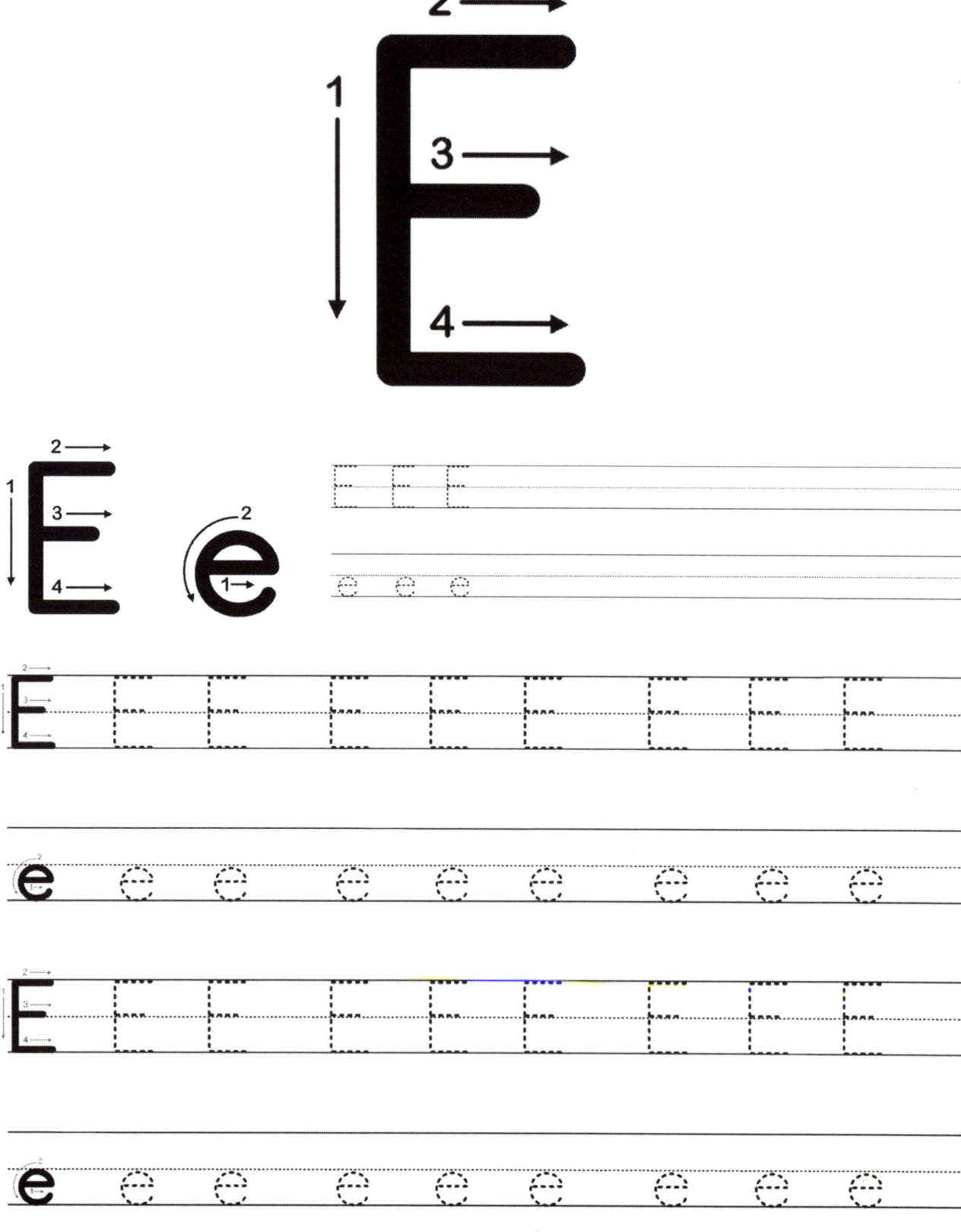

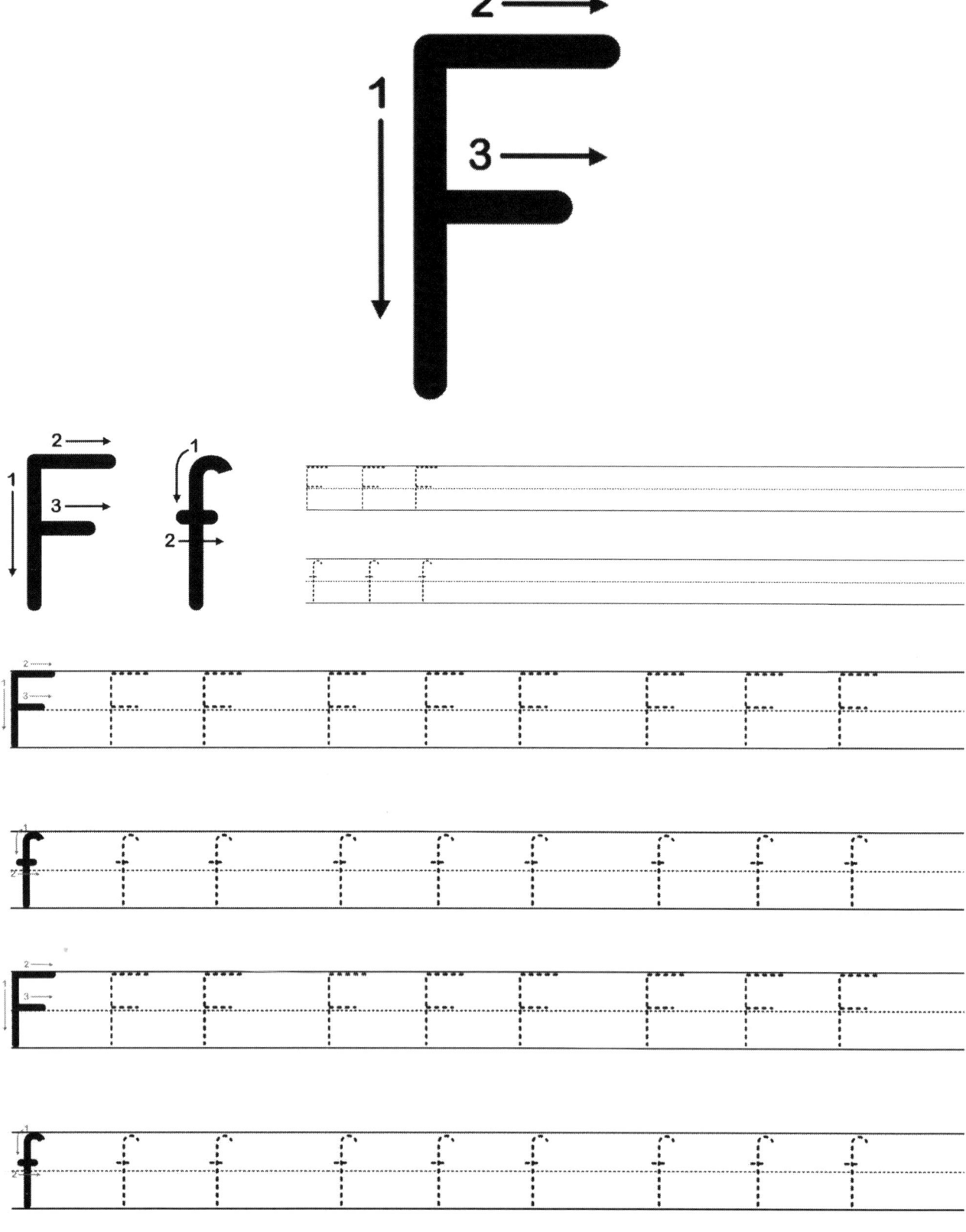

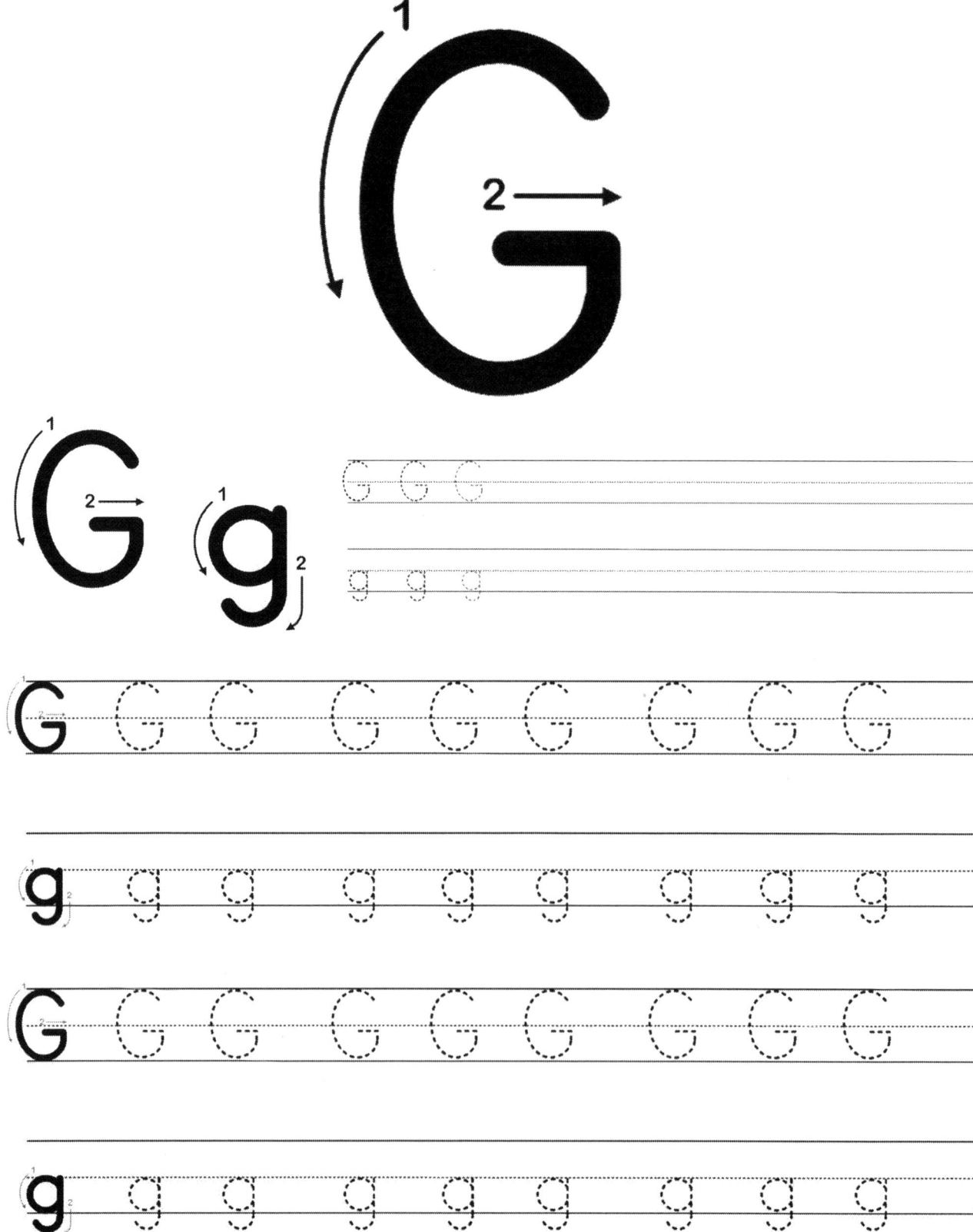

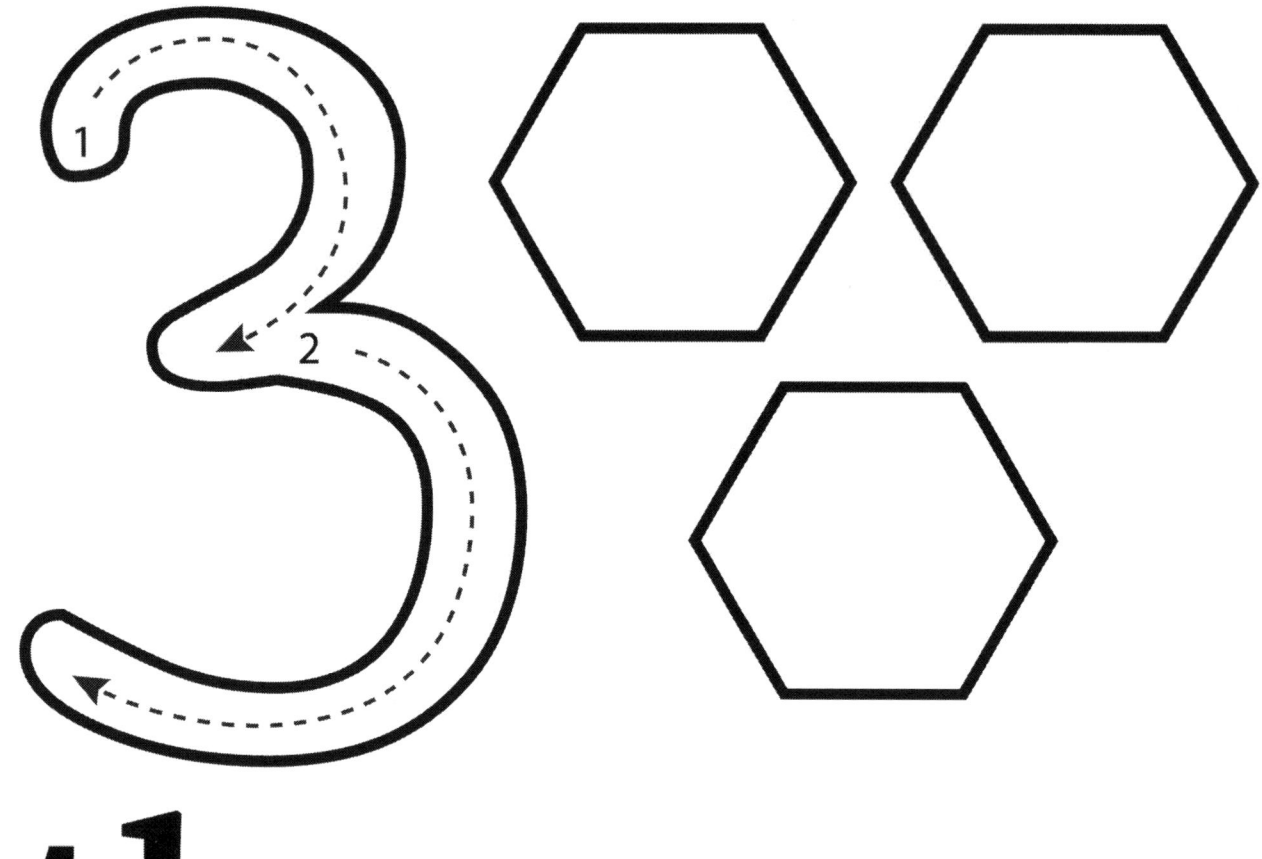

three

3 3 3 3 3

3 3 3 3 3

3 3 3 3 3

3 3 3 3 3

3 3 3 3 3

3 3 3 3 3

3 3 3 3 3

3 3 3 3 3

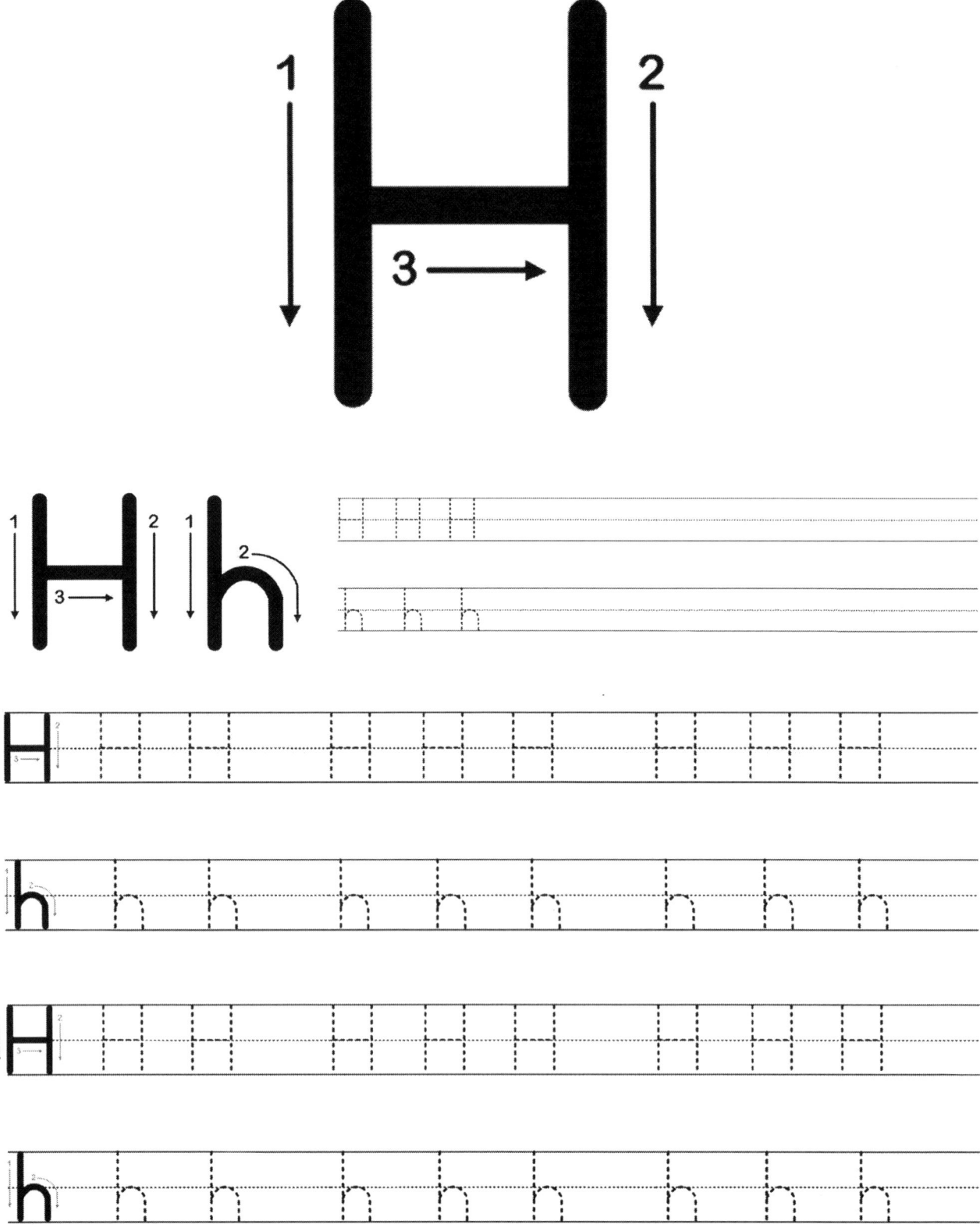

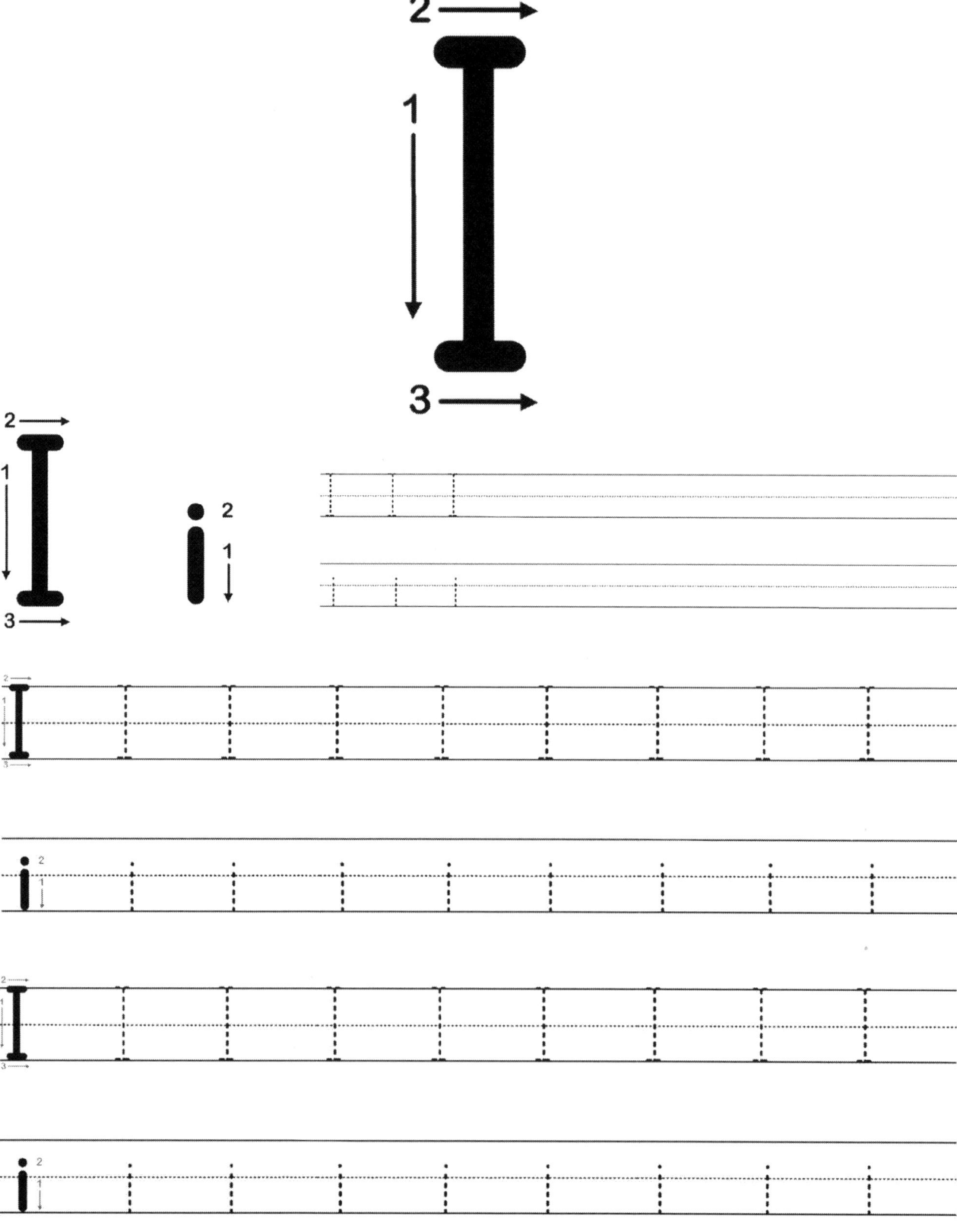

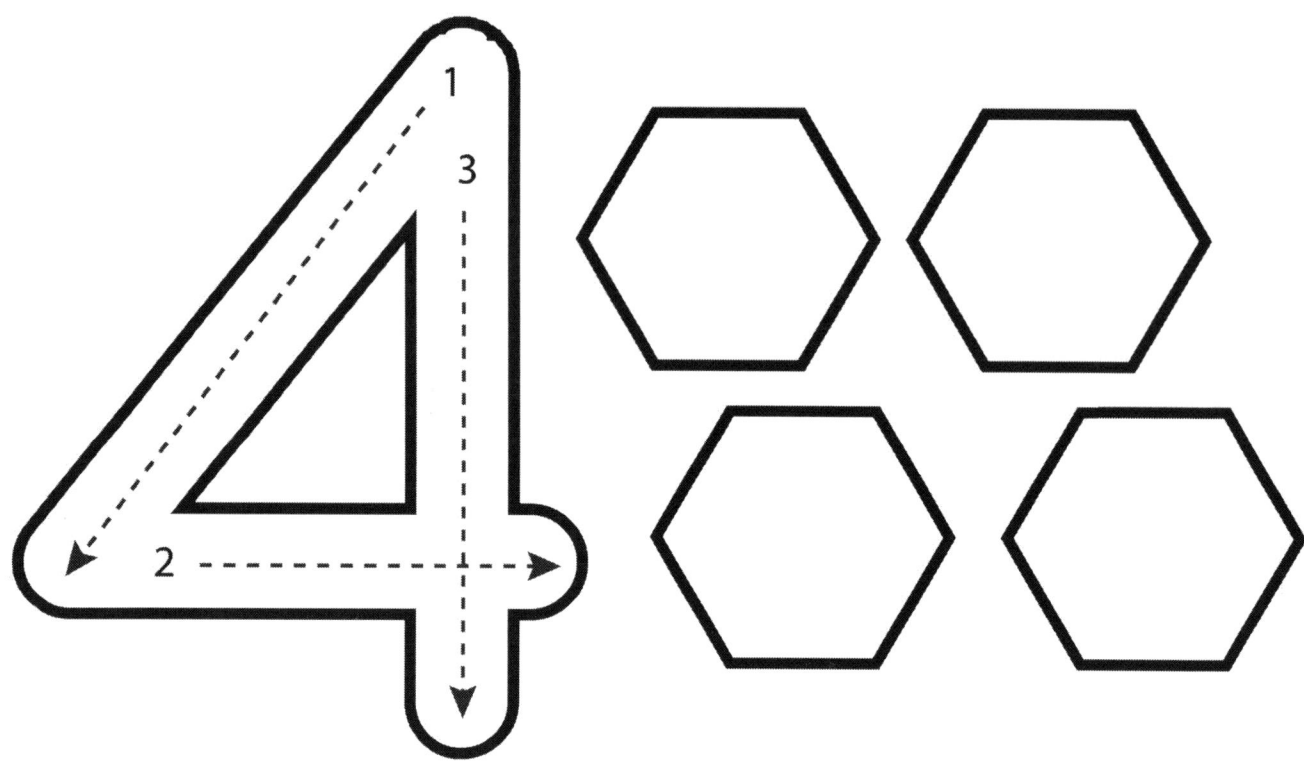

four

4 ⋯4⋯ ⋯4⋯ ⋯4⋯ ⋯4⋯

4 ⋯4⋯ ⋯4⋯ ⋯4⋯ ⋯4⋯

4   4 4 4 4

4   4 4 4 4

4   4 4 4 4

4   4 4 4 4

4   4 4 4 4

4   4 4 4 4

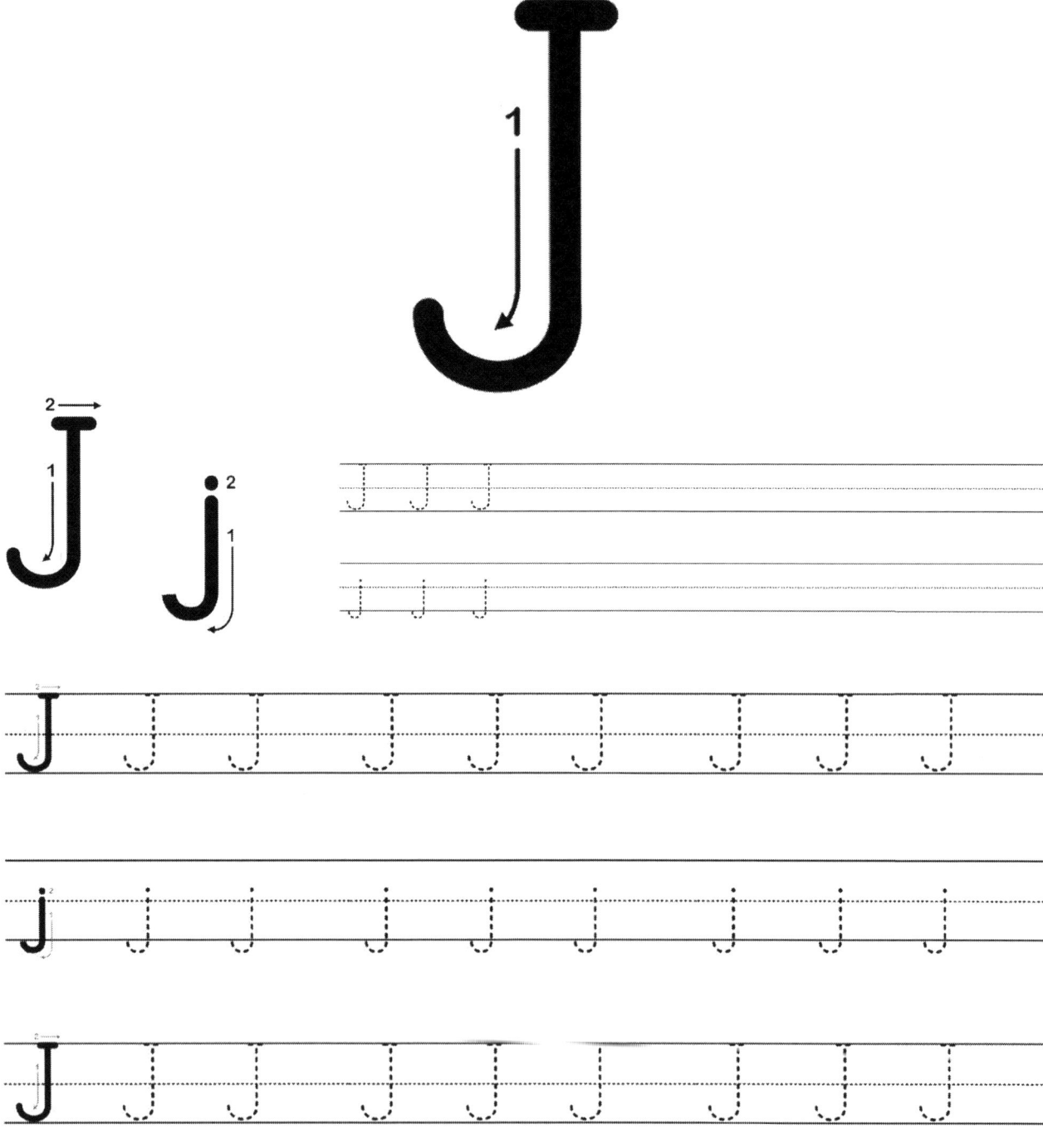

five

5　5　5　5　5

5　5　5　5　5

5　5　5　5　5

5　5　5　5　5

5　5　5　5　5

5　5　5　5　5

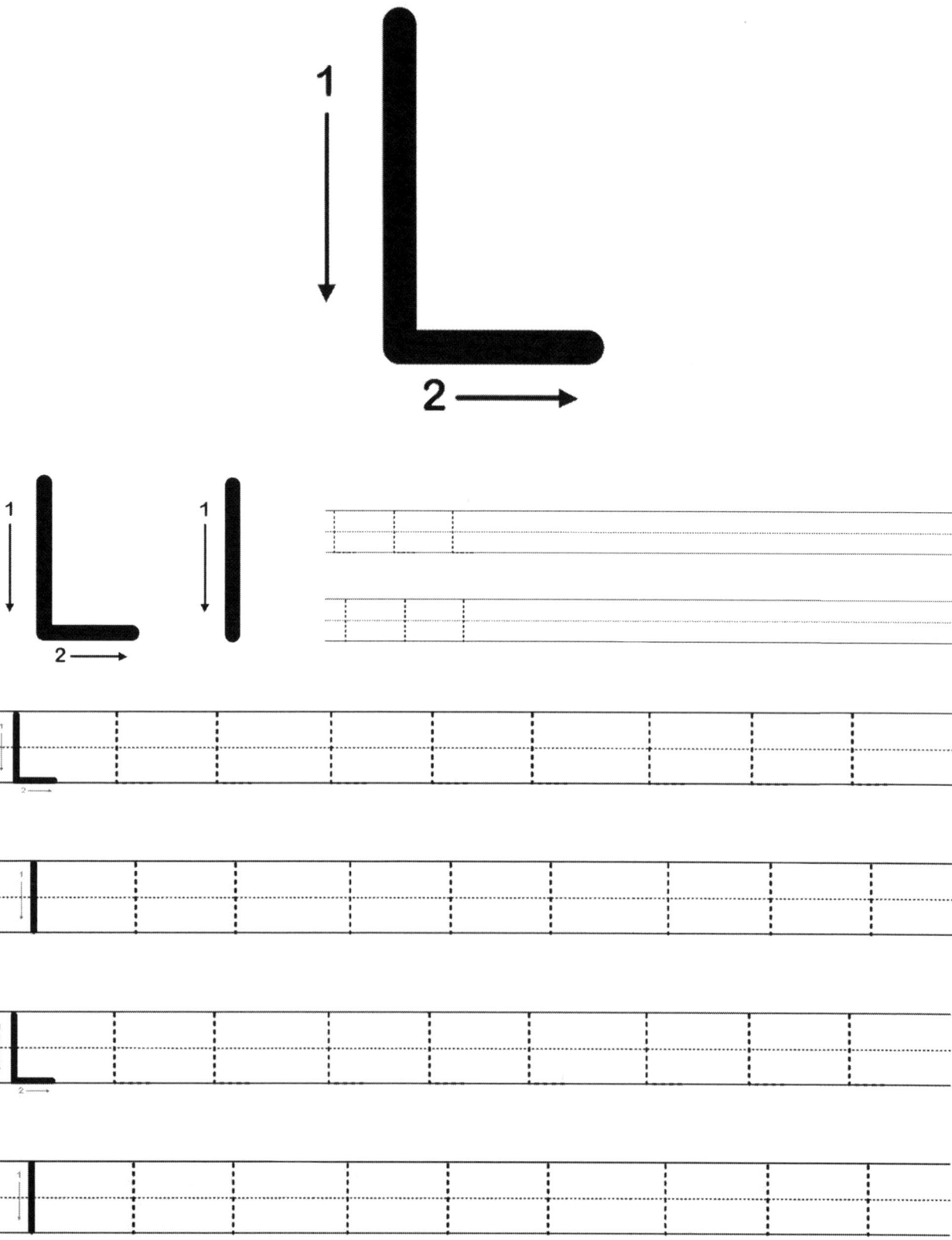

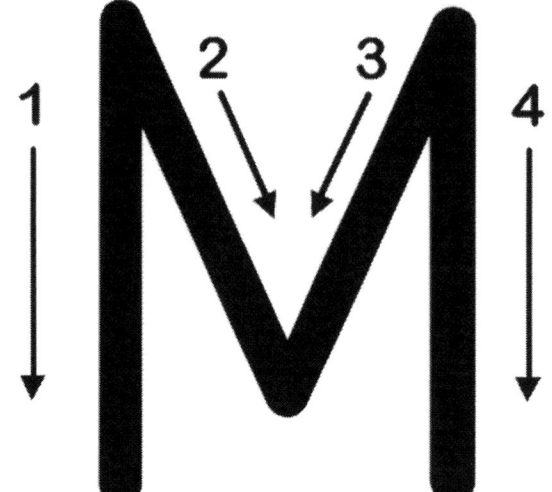

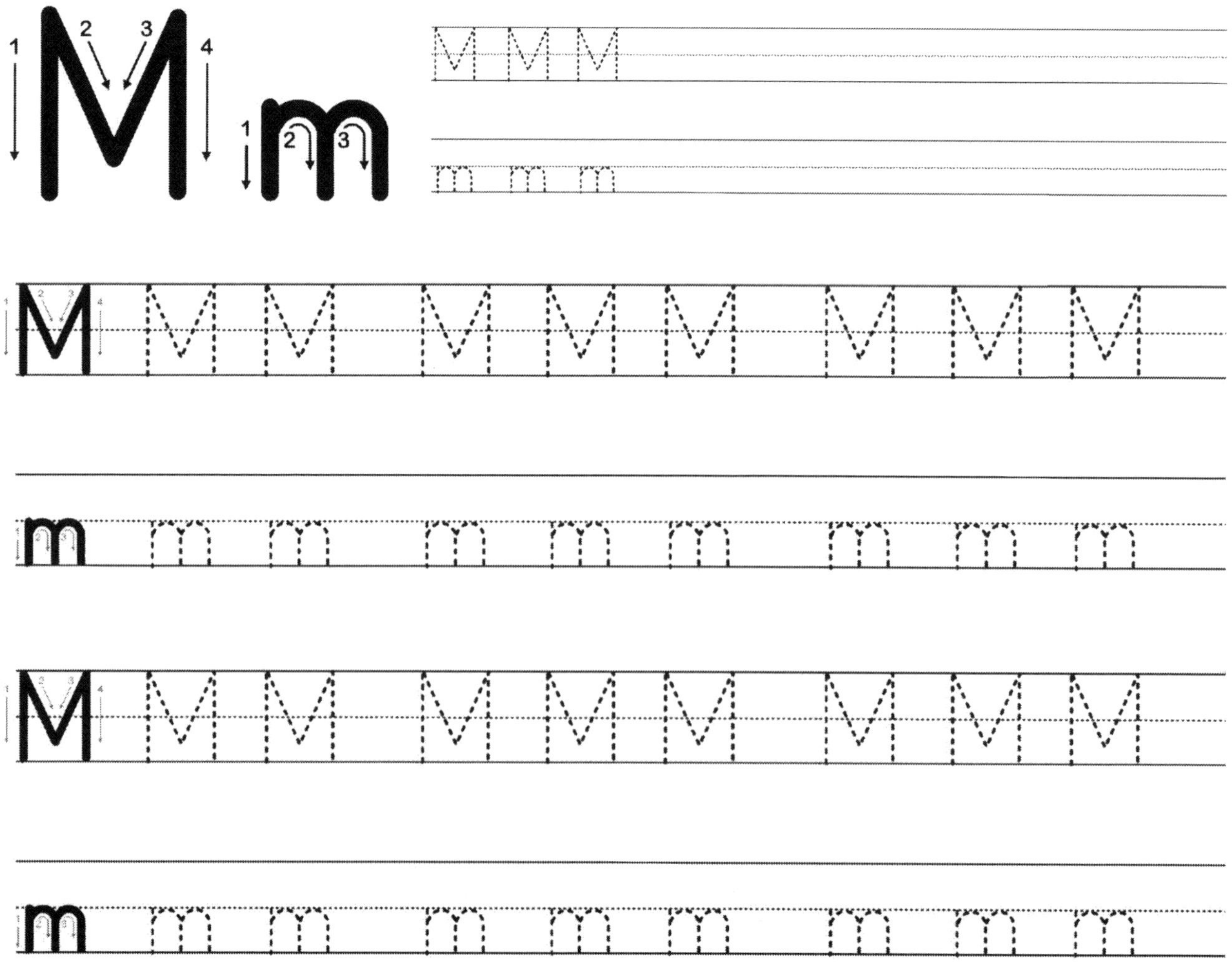

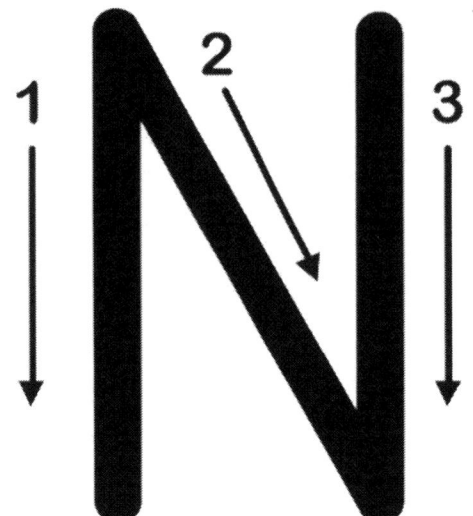

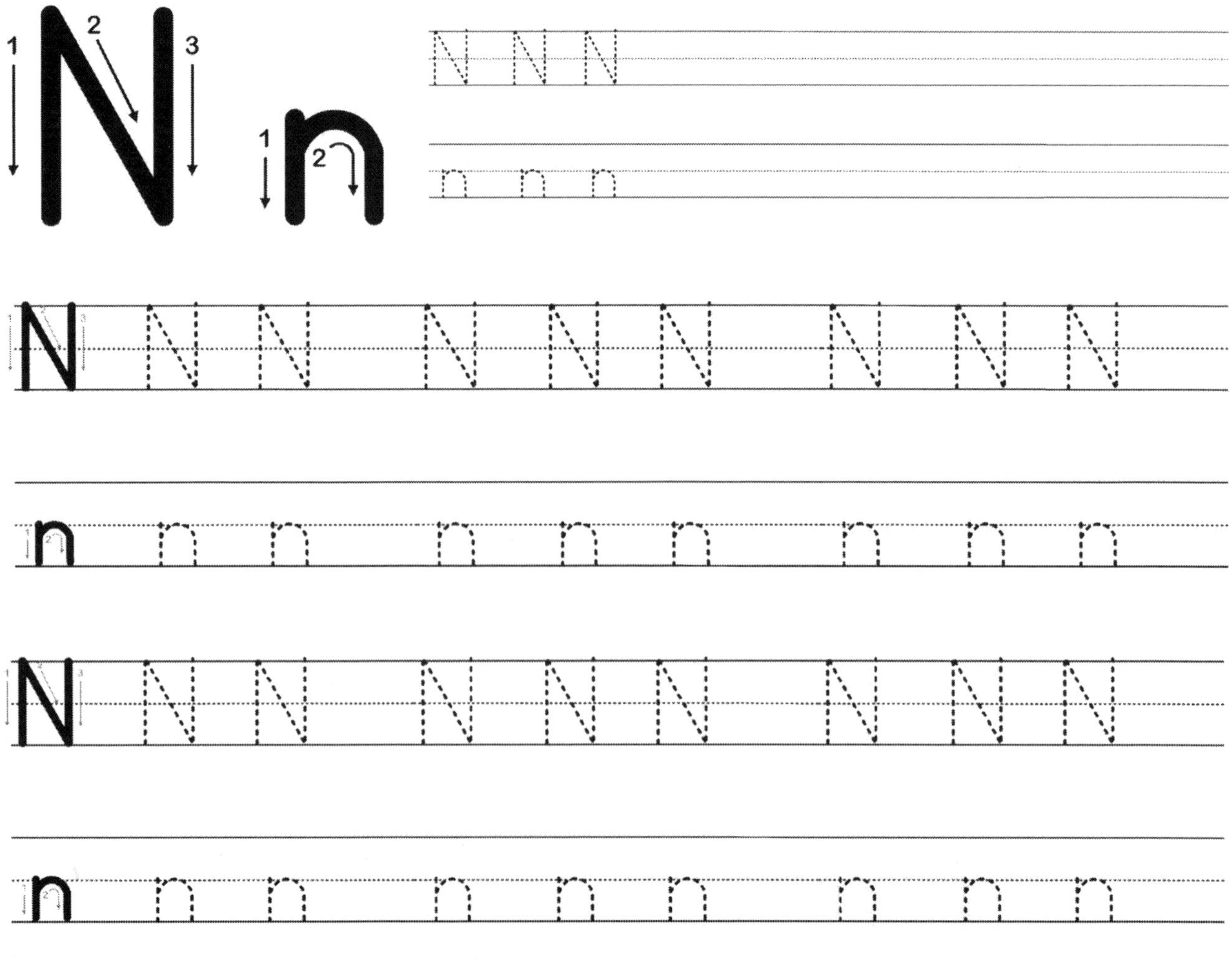

six

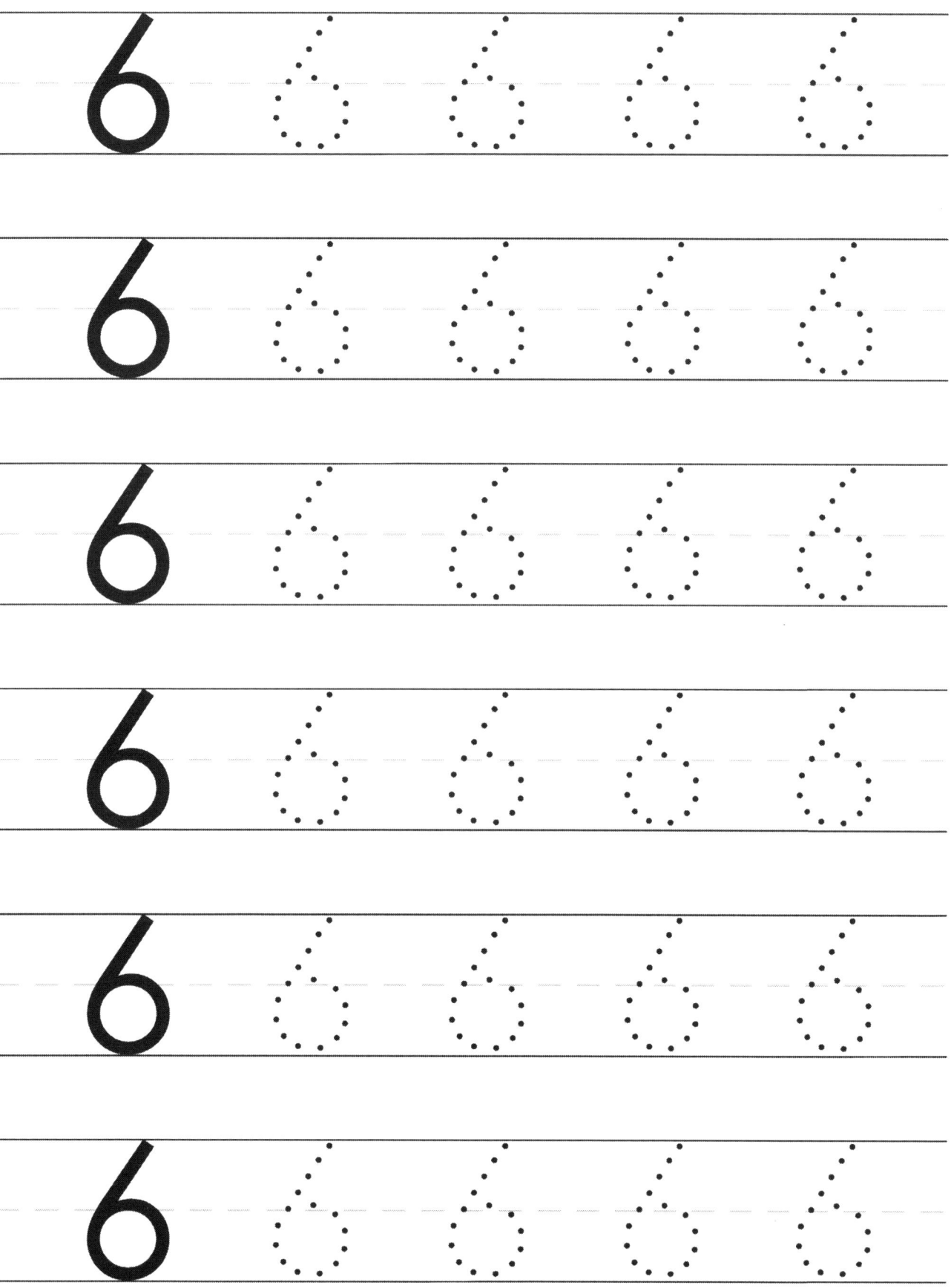

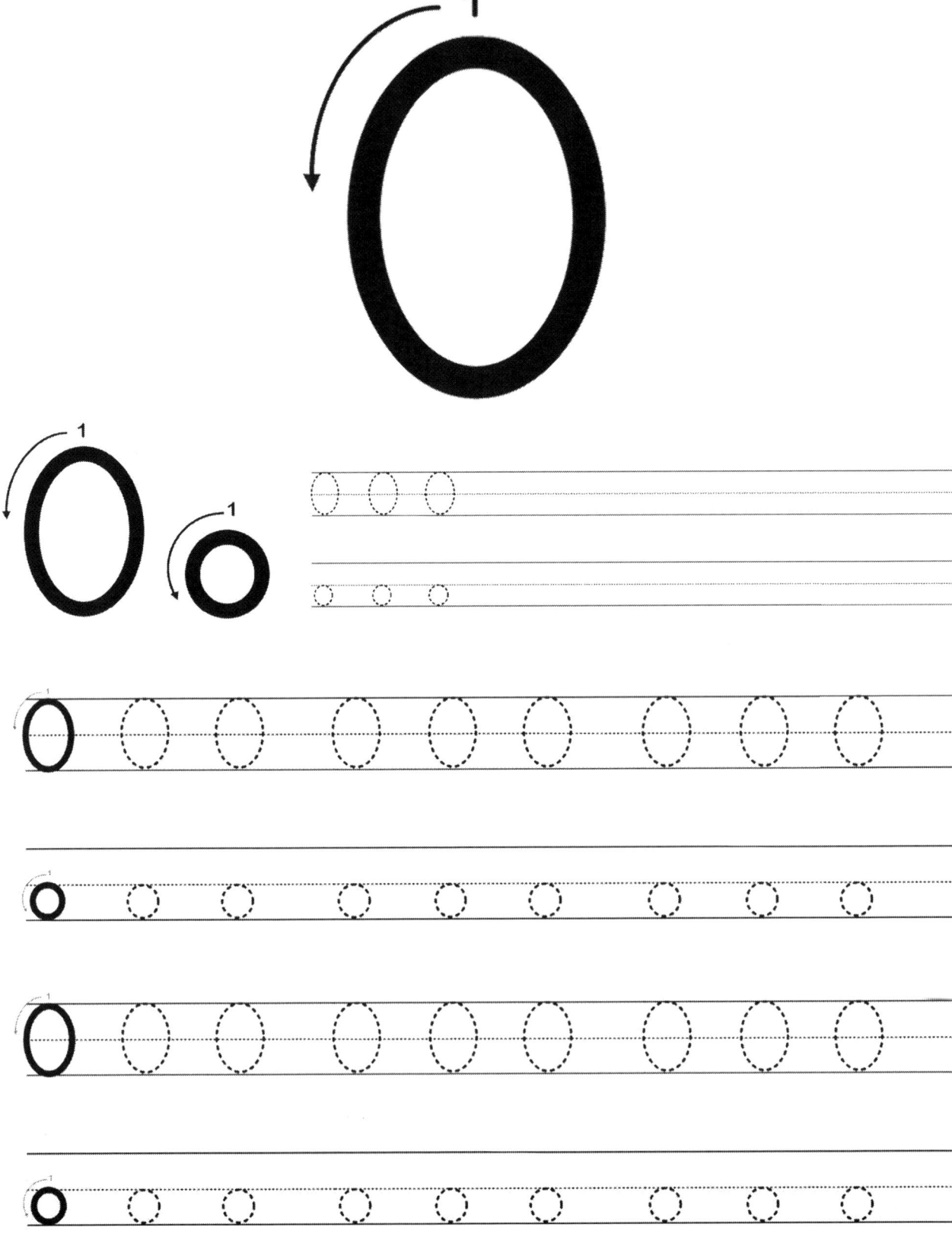

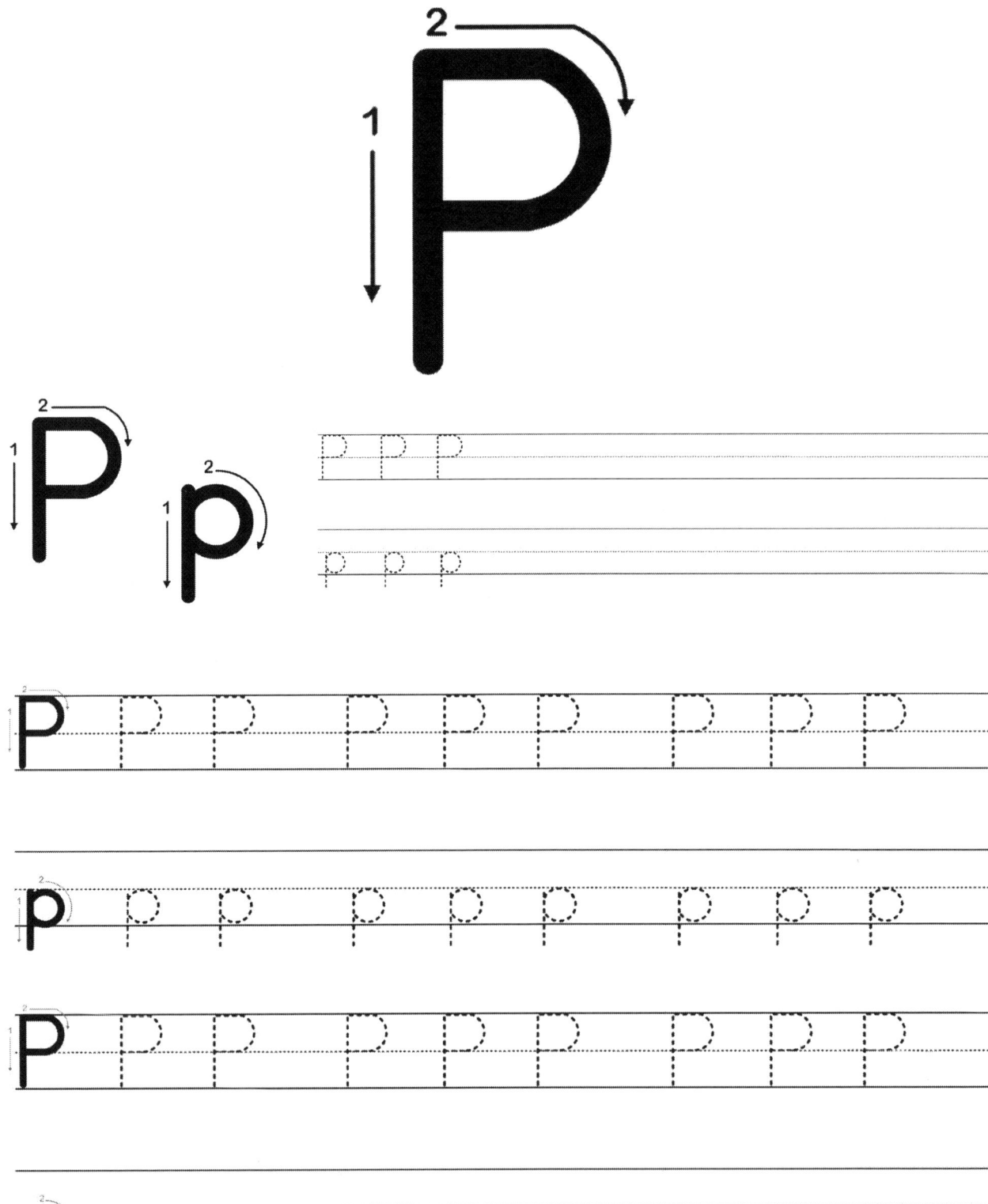

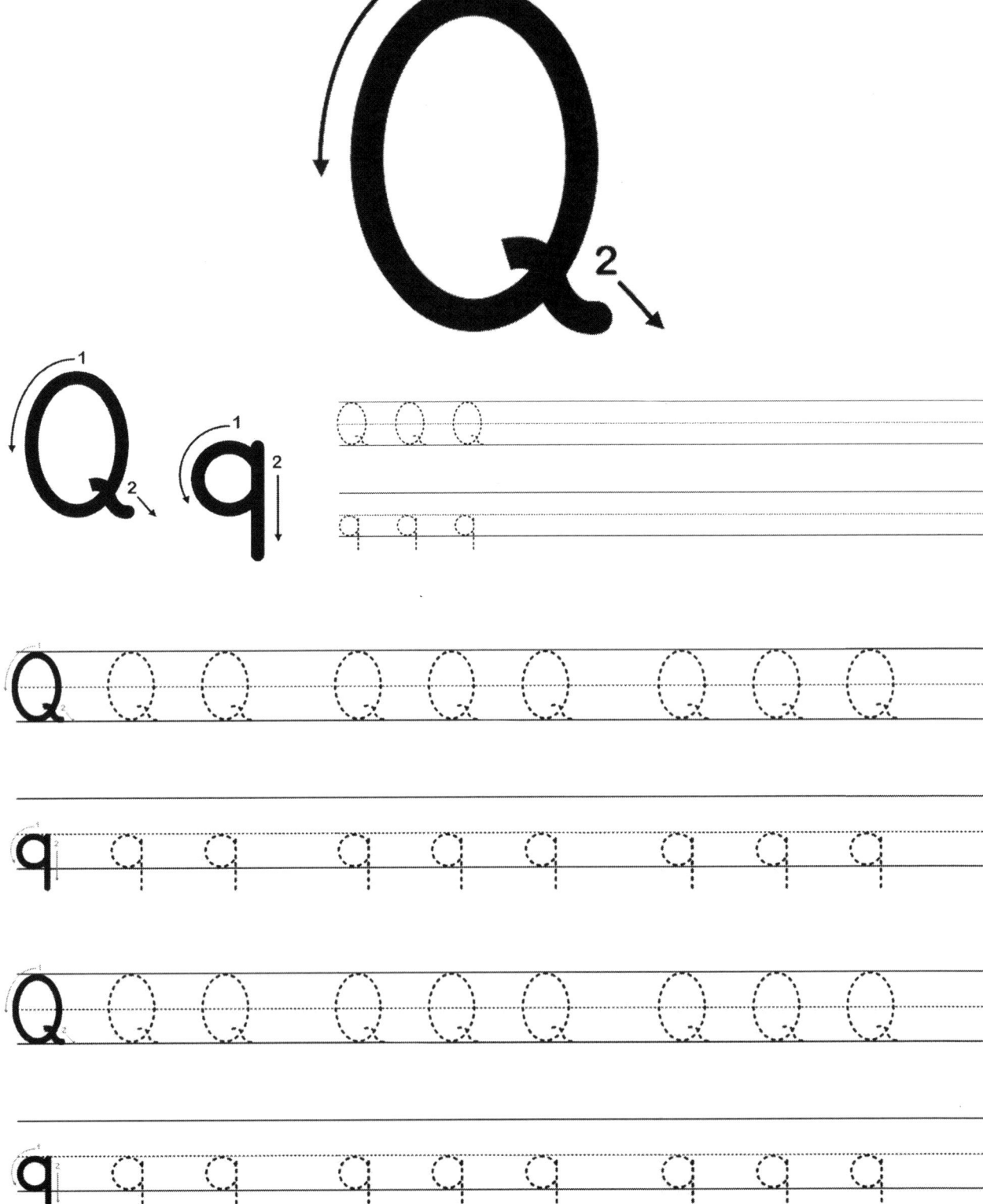

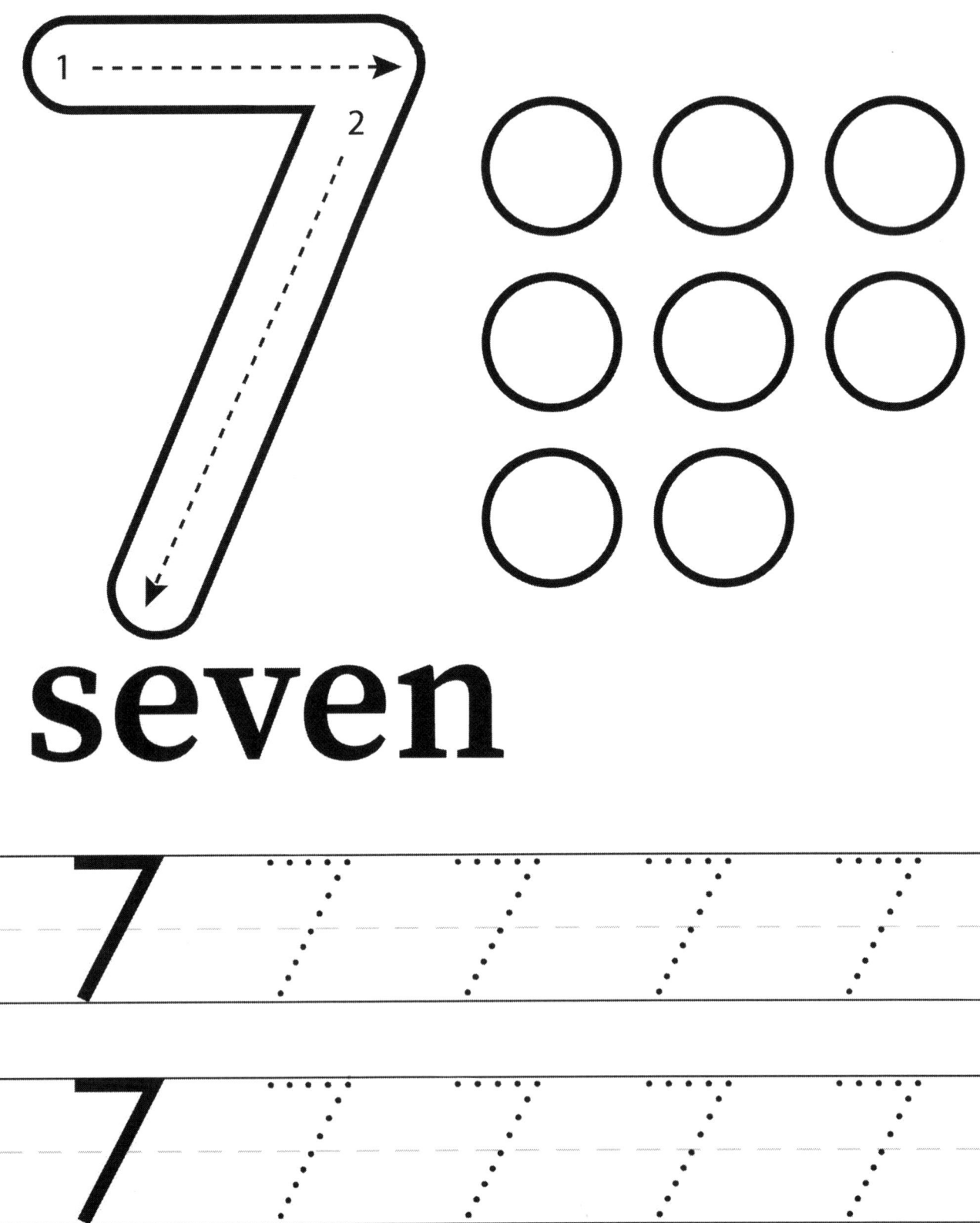
seven

7

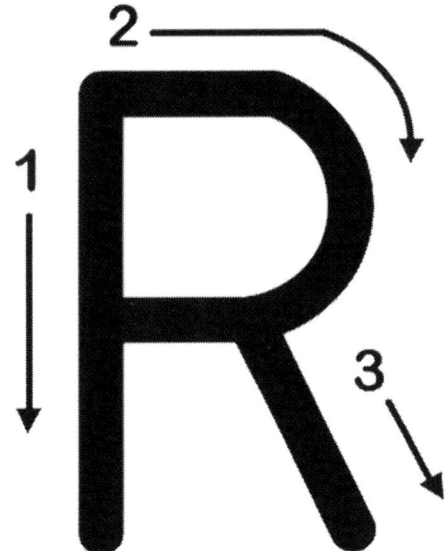

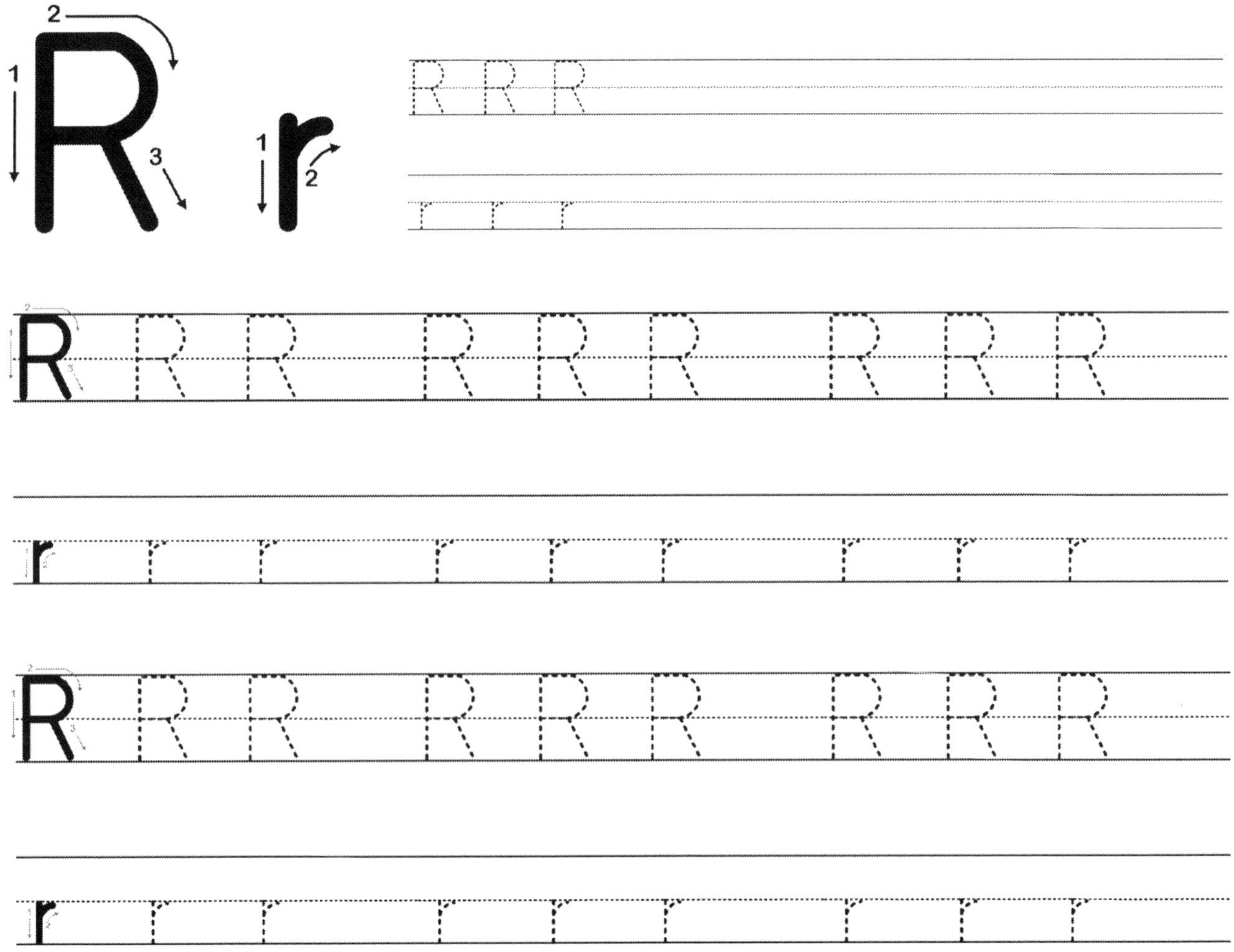

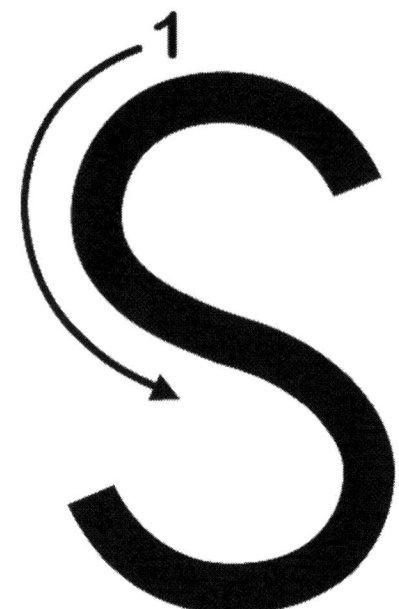

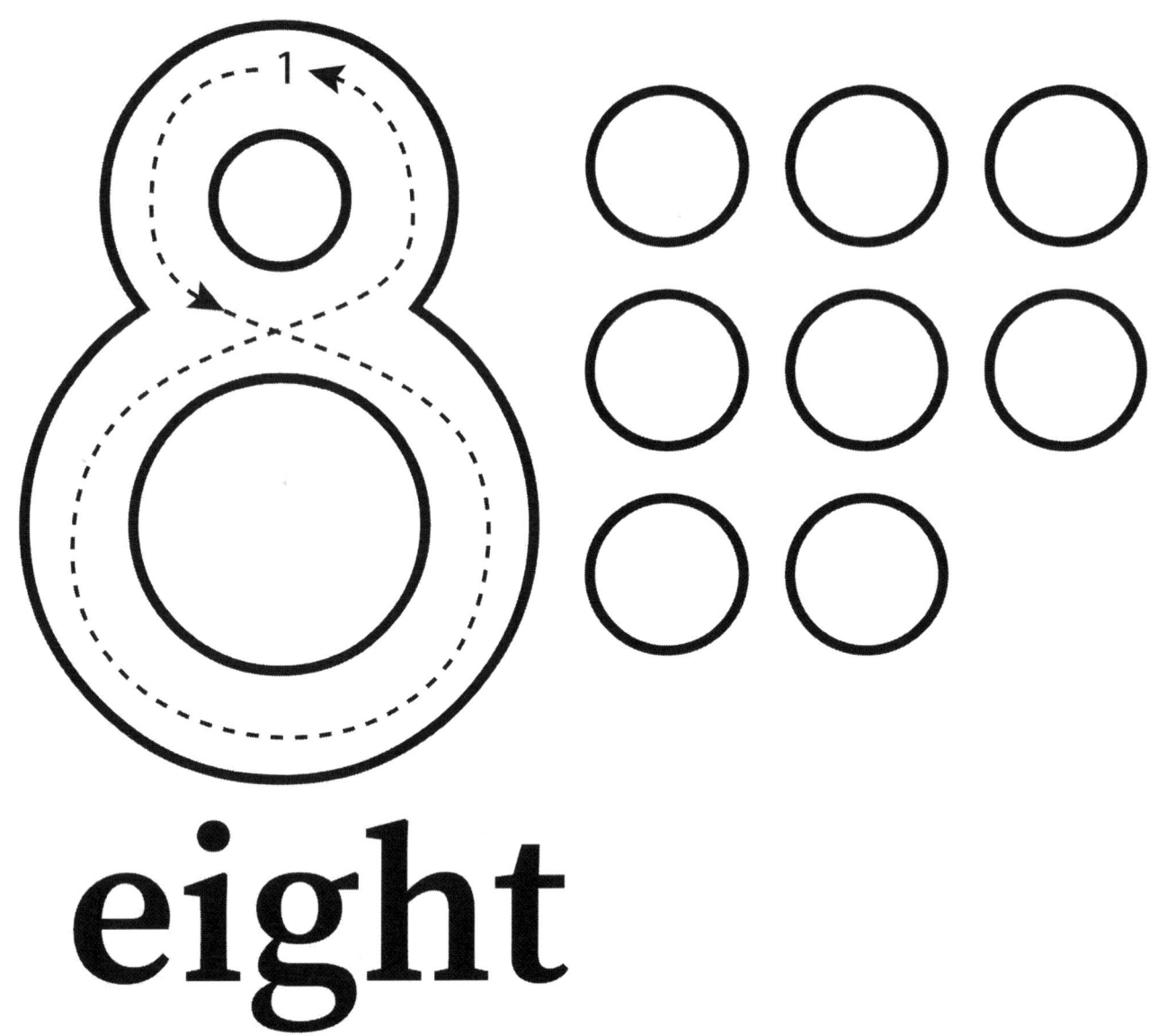

eight

8 8 8 8 8
8 8 8 8 8
8 8 8 8 8
8 8 8 8 8
8 8 8 8 8
8 8 8 8 8

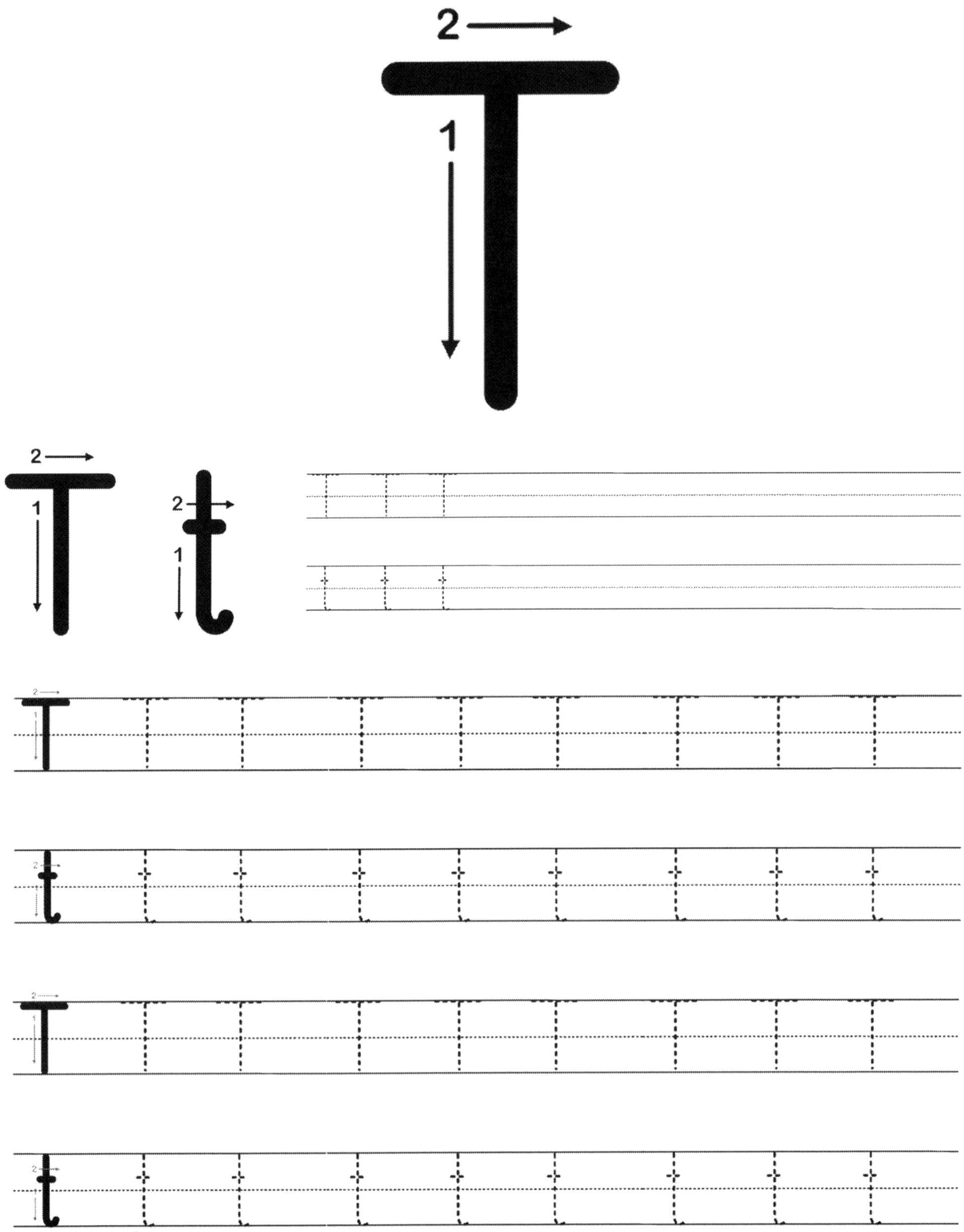

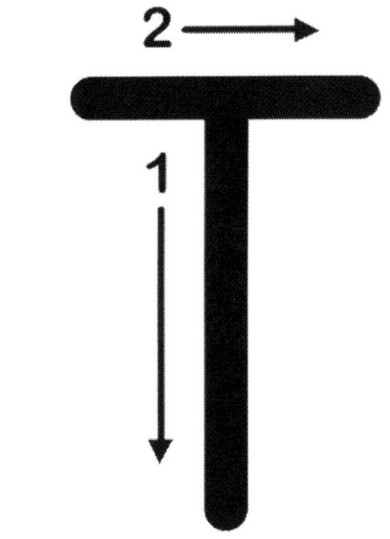

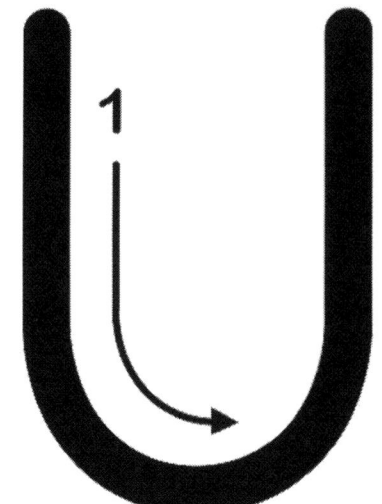

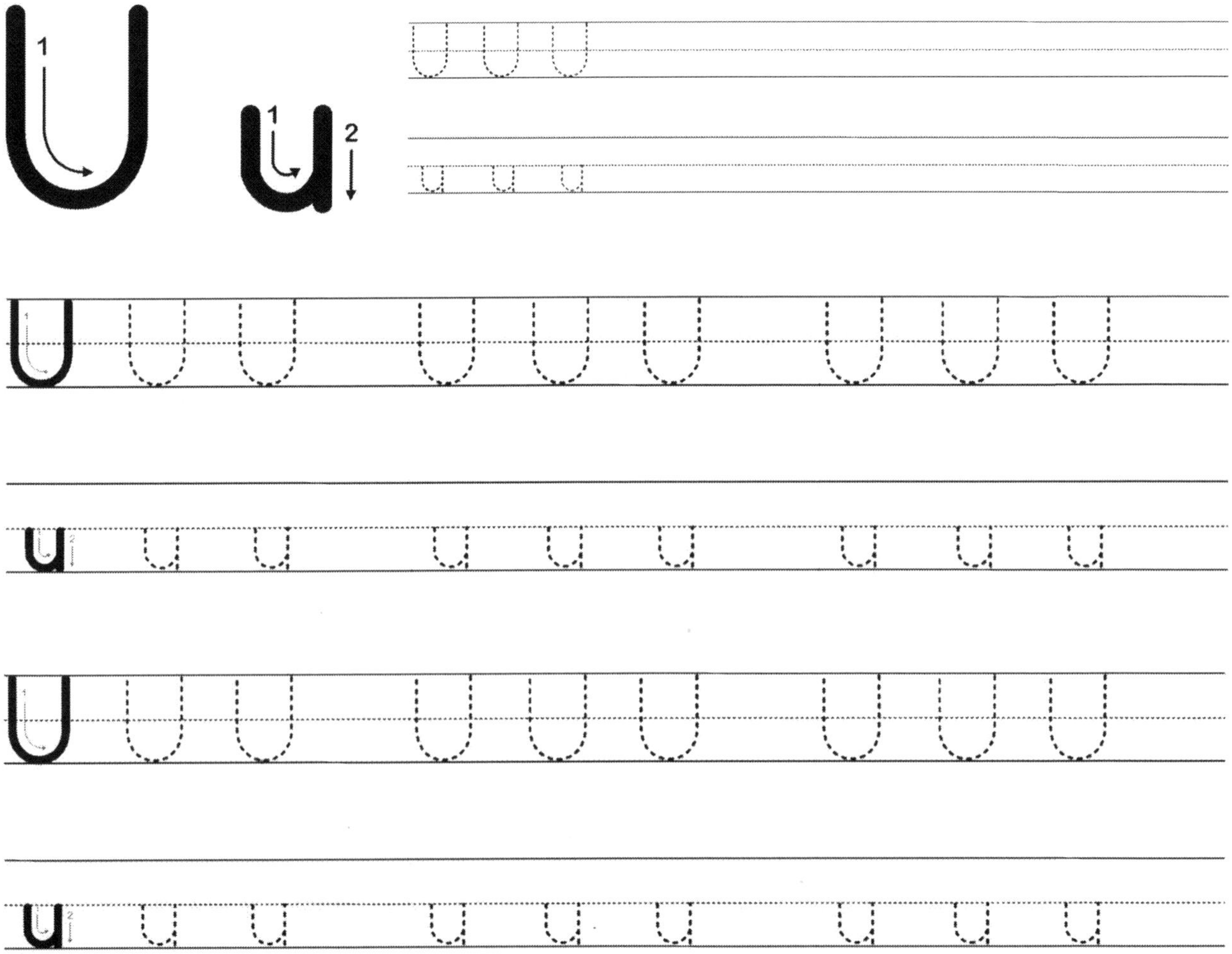

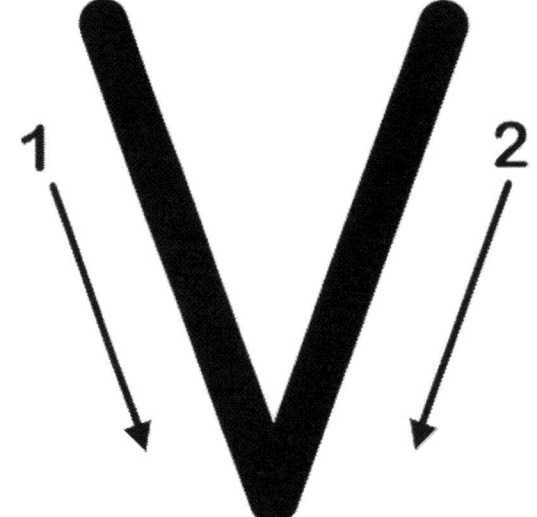

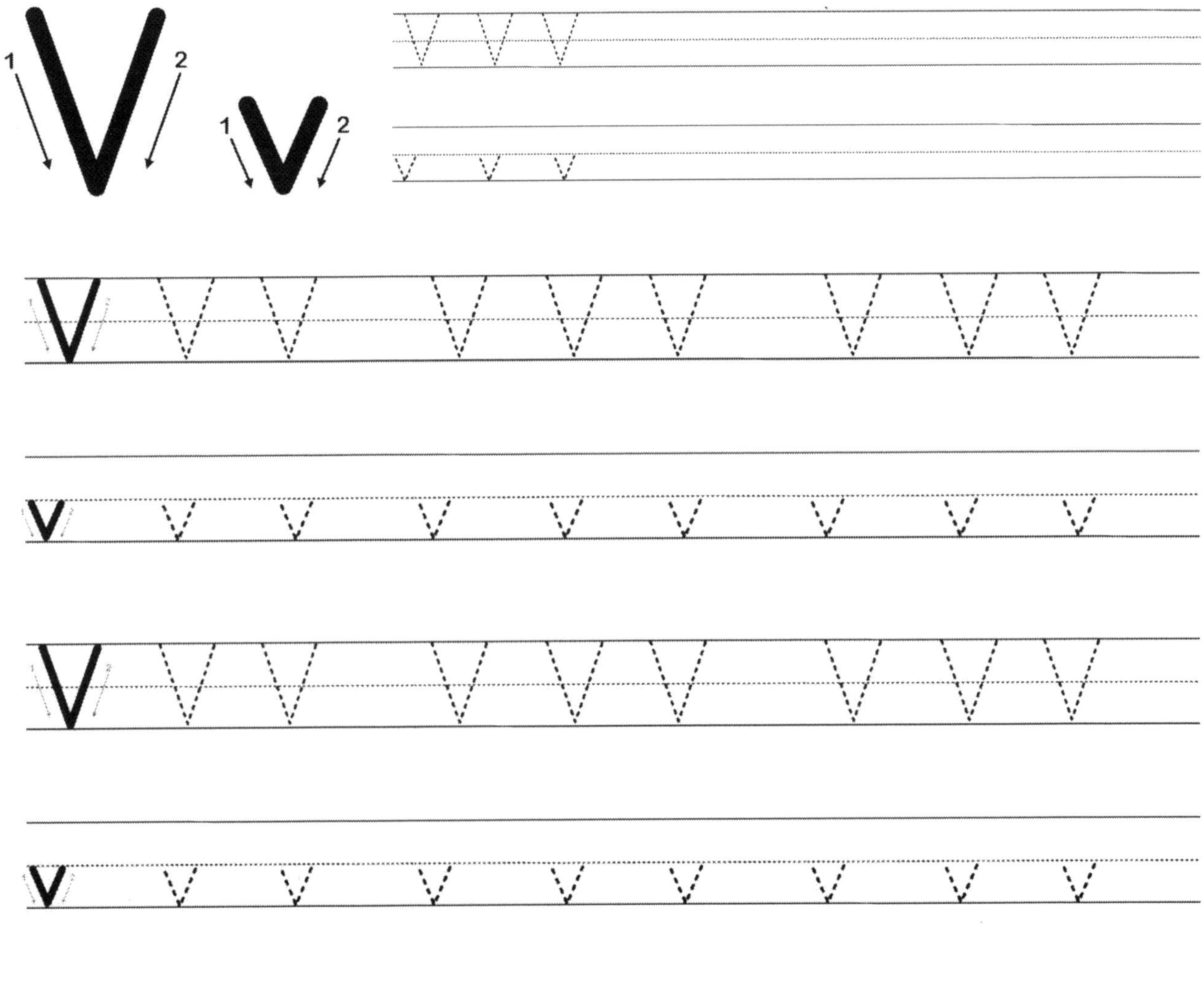

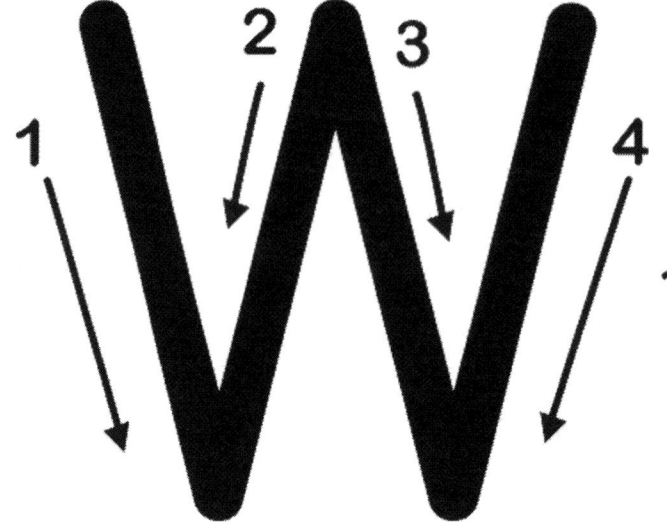
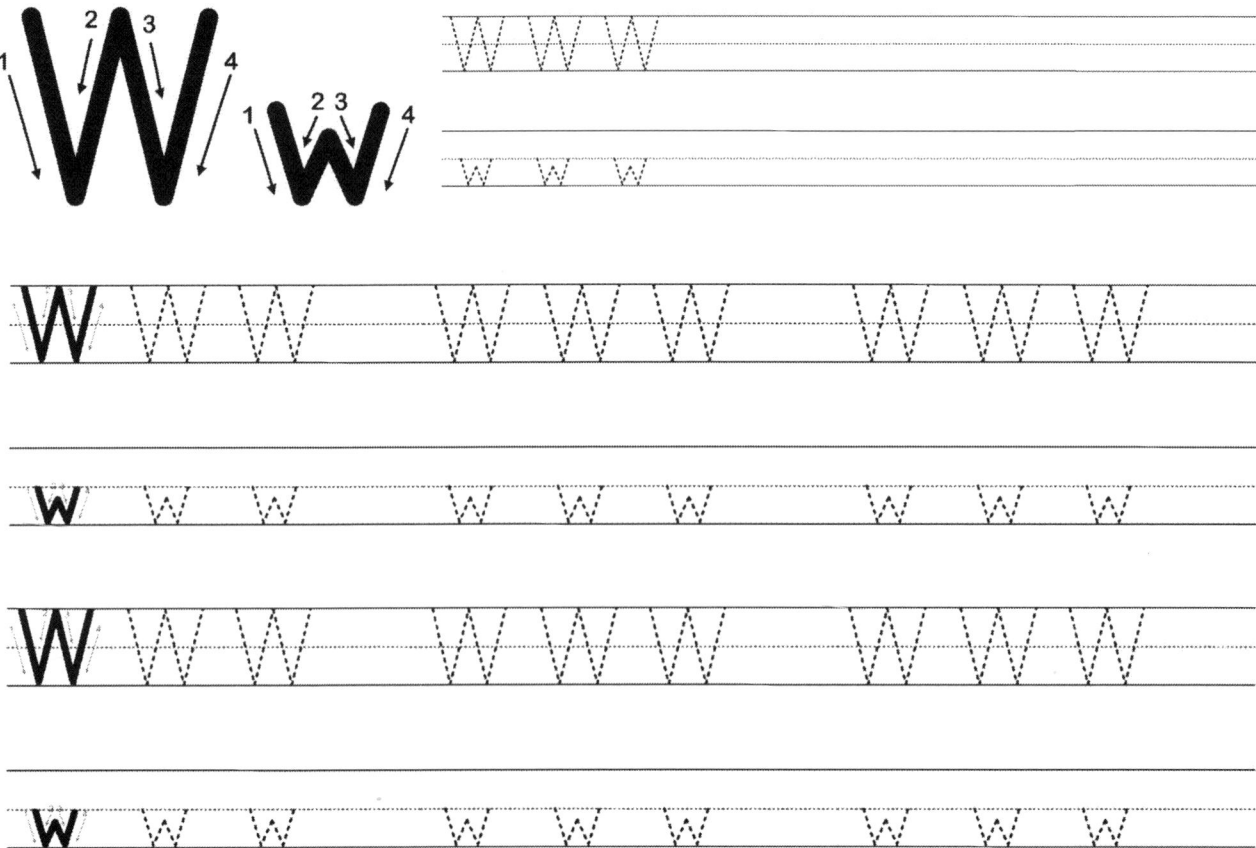

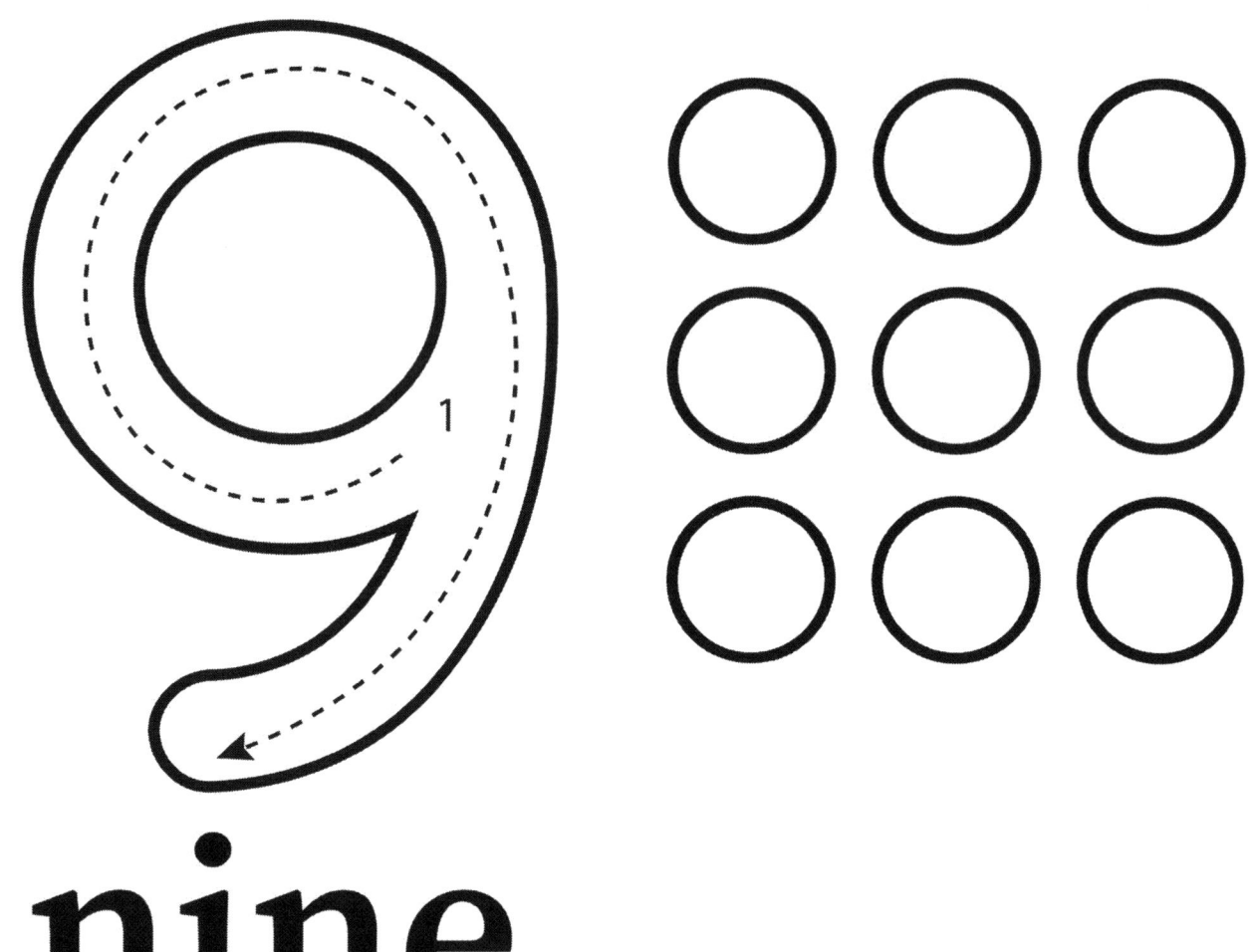

nine

9 9 9 9 9

9 9 9 9 9

9 9 9 9 9

9 9 9 9 9

9 9 9 9 9

9 9 9 9 9

10　10　10　10
10　10　10　10
10　10　10　10
10　10　10　10
10　10　10　10
10　10　10　10

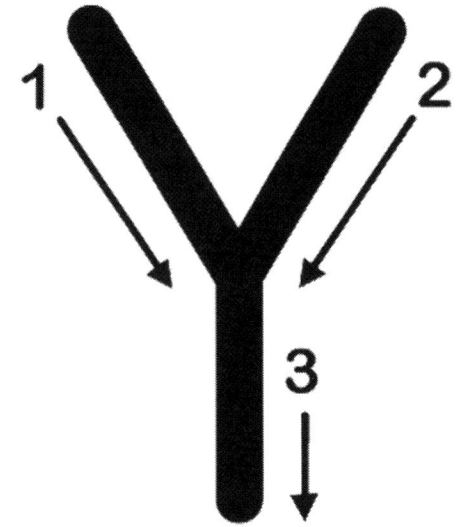

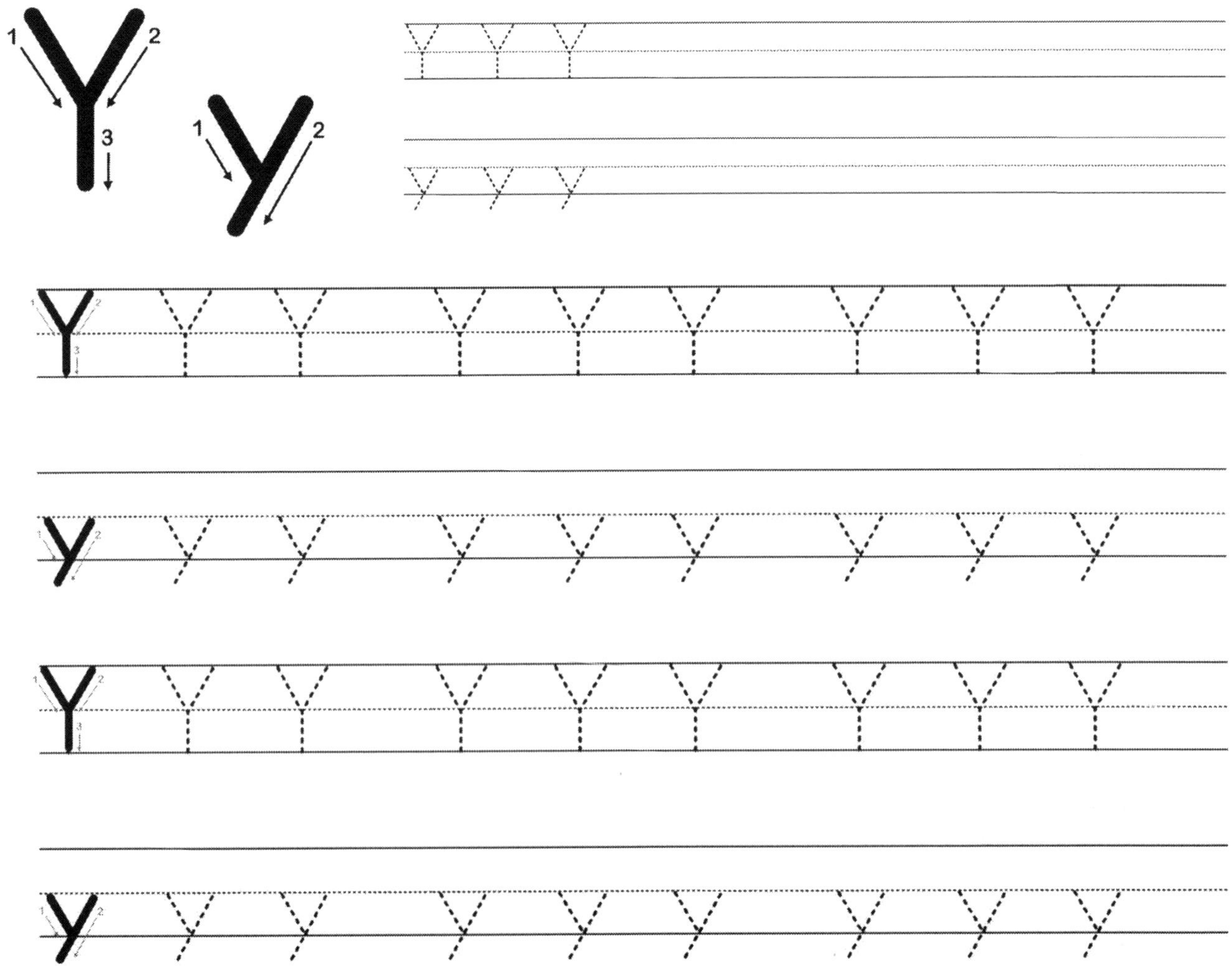

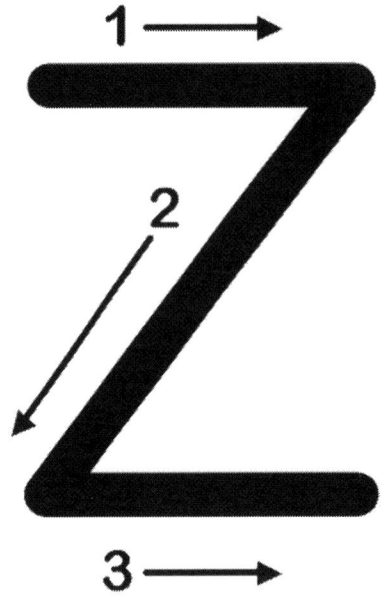

Alphabet & Numbers Tracing Chart

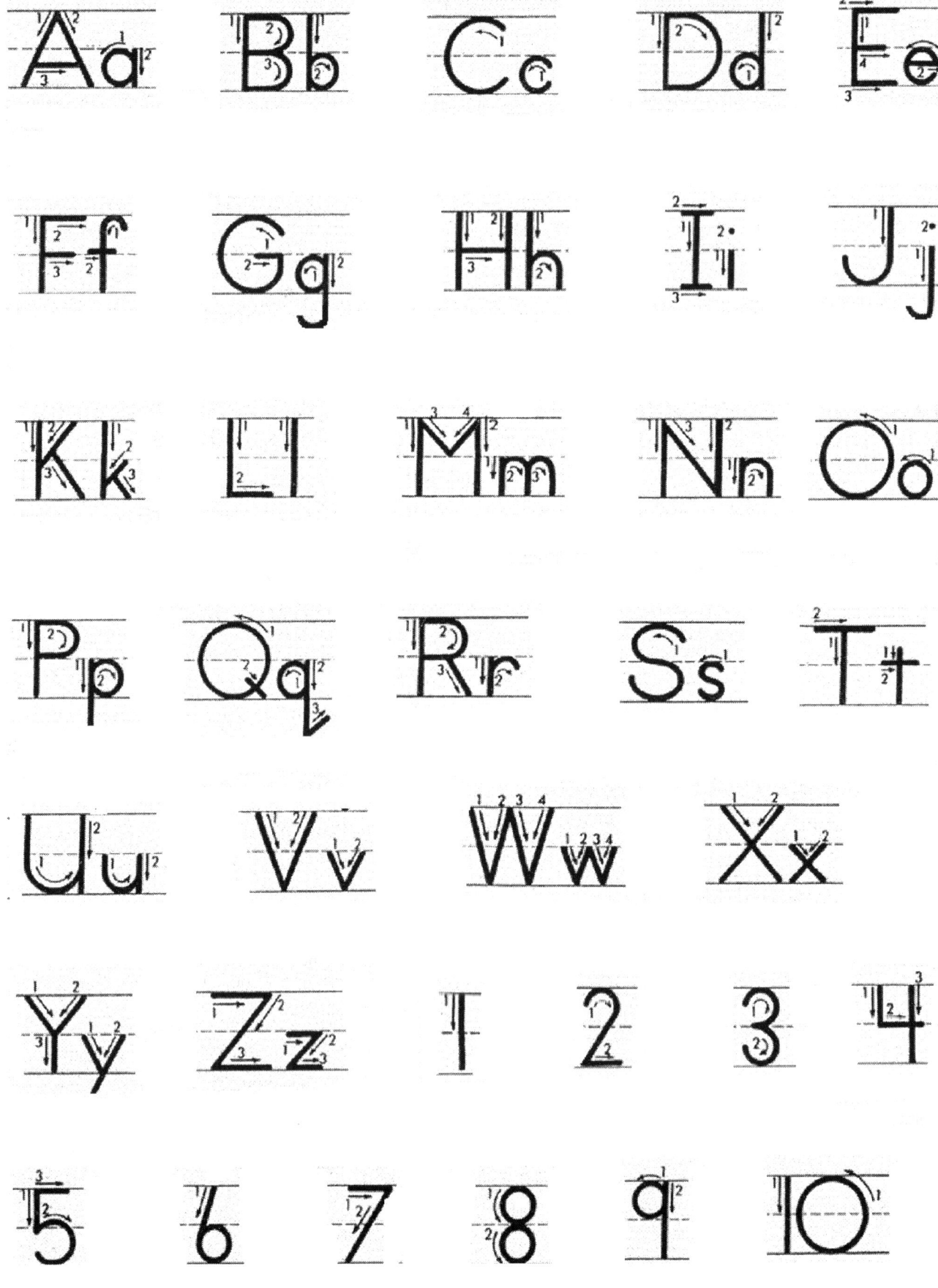

Thank you for your support. We hope you enjoyed your notebook. Scan the QR below to check out more titles like this one from Juju Journals.

Juju Journals
Jot down your thoughts

Printed in Dunstable, United Kingdom